SOME PROBLEMS OF THE CONSTITUTION

Politics

Editor

PROFESSOR W. A. ROBSON

B.SC(ECON), PH.D, LL.M

Professor Emeritus of Public Administration
in the University of London

SOME PROBLEMS OF THE CONSTITUTION

Geoffrey Marshall
Fellow of The Queen's College, Oxford
&
Graeme C. Moodie
Professor of Politics in the University of York

HUTCHINSON UNIVERSITY LIBRARY
LONDON

HUTCHINSON & CO (*Publishers*) LTD
3 Fitzroy Square, London W1

London Melbourne Sydney Auckland
Wellington Johannesburg Cape Town
and agencies throughout the world

First published 1959
Second edition 1961
Third edition 1964
Fourth (revised) edition 1967
Reprinted 1968
Fifth (revised) edition 1971

The design on the cover of the paperback edition shows an extract from a Royal Commission of Assent of 1910 (George V) with its wafer seal superimposed. Edward VII's Seal continued to be used until 1911

This book has been set in Times type, printed in Great Britain on smooth wove paper by Anchor Press, and bound by Wm. Brendon, both of Tiptree, Essex

ISBN 0 09 109940 4 (cased)
0 09 109941 2 (paper)

The amount of time that people are willing to waste in hearing each other talk is a very important constituent of our political life.

SIR OLIVER FRANKS

(*Committee on Administrative Tribunals and Enquiries Minutes of Evidence. Day 24*)

CONTENTS

PREFACE TO FIRST EDITION

Since the United Kingdom, despite the inconvenience caused to foreign students of our government, refuses to enact a Constitution, constitutional questions are often a matter of argument about the interpretation of general principles or political precedents. In the late nineteenth century Dicey discerned and publicised two such principles —the supremacy of Parliament and the rule of law. In the day-to-day working of government in the twentieth century the principle of ministerial responsibility (to which *Dicey's Law of the Constitution* gives little detailed attention) has assumed equally obvious importance. In one sense much of the constitutional history of the present century might be represented as a conflict between this and the two former principles. We have tried, therefore, both to illustrate the way in which argument about the rules of constitutional behaviour is carried on and to set out the problems raised by the principle of ministerial responsibility, looking in turn at the relations of Ministers with the Crown, Parliament, the courts, the administration, and the public. In teaching British government we have found that the works of political historians on the one hand and those of lawyers writing for lawyers on the other, leave a gap which students sometimes find hard to bridge. In addition much new information and argument about the role of the administration and the control of ministerial discretion has recently emerged from the evidence given before the Franks Committee and the adoption by the Government of its Report. It seemed that there might therefore be some usefulness both to the general reader and to undergraduates beginning the study of British government in a short account of some of the questions posed by political and administrative change in the Constitution.

There are of course many excellent descriptive works on the general structure of British government and we have both assumed and presumed upon their existence in selecting issues for discussion.

What might seem to others equally urgent questions have been omitted and we must invoke whatever protection from censure is afforded by the prefacing of our problems with an indefinite article.

We are grateful to the editors of *Public Administration, Public Law* and *Parliamentary Affairs* for permission to include several passages containing material which originally appeared in those journals. For criticism and most valuable suggestions for improving (and purging) the manuscript we are greatly indebted to Professor Wilfrid Harrison, and to many colleagues in Oxford and Glasgow. For what remains we are jointly culpable.

NOTE TO FIFTH EDITION

In this edition developments since 1967 are noted. Since the First edition an important change has taken place in the machinery and conventions governing the selection of the Prime Minister (Chapter 3). Two matters particularly affecting the responsibilities of ministers are the growth of specialised committees in the House of Commons (Chapter 8) and the enactment of the Parliamentary Commissioner legislation of 1967 (Chapters 6 and 8). Of other detectable tendencies, one has been a less assertive attitude of the House of Commons towards it privileges and a more assertive attitude by the courts towards the exercise of administrative powers.

G.M.
G.C.M.

I

THE CONSTITUTION

1. *The sources of the Constitution*

It has always been difficult to give accurate descriptions of British constitutional practices. One reason is simply that it is hard to describe traditions. Patterns of behaviour which are influenced by tradition may be changing whilst the tradition is being identified. Moreover, inner changes may be partly concealed by the persistence of traditional forms. 'An ancient and ever-altering Constitution,' Walter Bagehot wrote in 1867, 'is like an old man who still wears with attached fondness clothes in the fashion of his youth: what you see of him is the same; what you do not see is wholly altered.'[1] Traditional legal forms in particular may be misleading guides to the facts of current constitutional behaviour. Professor A. V. Dicey, whose *Introduction to the Study of the Law of the Constitution* first appeared in 1885, complained, for example, in the opening chapters of his book that legal textbooks sometimes contained accounts of constitutional law which were 'a kind of maze in which the wanderer is perplexed by unreality'. In Blackstone's *Commentaries on the Laws of England*, Dicey said, students might read that the Constitution concentrated all executive power in the hands of the King. 'The language of this passage,' he remarked, 'is impressive. . . . It has but one fault; the statements it contains are the direct opposite of the truth.'[2] Part of the difficulty involved in stating accurately the current facts about the Constitution flows of course from the notorious, and perhaps unfortunate, fact that no official collection of constitutional rules exists in this country. There is no formal document or set of statutes dignified with the title. Elsewhere—in the United States for example —there is less trouble about this. The constitution is set out in a document which, it is said, can be read (if not necessarily understood) in

1. *The English Constitution* (OUP ed. 1928), p. 1.
2. *Introduction to the Study of the Law of the Constitution* (10th ed.), pp. 7–9.

about twenty minutes. But in Britain each commentator has to make his own selection of rules and practices which he may consider to be of 'constitutional' importance. The consequences are, of course, academic rather than practical. It is not clear what sort of answer the average Englishman would give if approached in the street and asked to say what form the Constitution took. But consider the unhappy plight of any compiler of an encyclopedia of the world's constitutions. A Frenchman in this position might simply omit the United Kingdom altogether on the ground that the British Constitution does not exist. An Englishman might do the same and comfort himself with the reflection that the Constitution 'is not written down in books, but . . . is found in the minds and practice of each generation'.[1]

Attempts in constitutional treatises to compare British institutions with 'formal' and documentary constitutions do certainly present an appearance of incongruity. One fairly recent constitutional encyclopedia, for example, sets out in the form of a table constitutional provisions in the various countries relating to the 'Form of Government', the 'Rights of the People', and the 'Source of Sovereign Power'. Under the last heading the entries for South Africa, the USSR, and Great Britain are respectively 'Almighty God', 'The Working People of Town and Country', and 'The Crown and the People'.[2] Since, in the case of Great Britain, the source of sovereign power is nowhere specified, the author had to make his own deduction, and to decide whether to give a legal or a political description (though the Crown plus the People appears to be not quite either). Others might disagree. They might for example say 'The Crown', or 'The Queen-in-Parliament', or 'The Electorate', or the 'House of Commons', since 'source' could be interpreted in terms of history, of law, of political theory, or of political facts.

2. *'The People'*

It has become an elementary commonplace that the emanation of sovereign power from the people of the United Kingdom, and its conferring upon Parliament, is a fact to which the Constitution itself is blind. With the exception of one brief period in English history (when Cromwell's Instrument of Government of 1653 declared the legislative power to reside in the person of the Lord Protector 'and the people') the authority of the nation has never been formally recognised as it has been in other constitutional systems. In the eye of the law there is only the Queen, her Ministers, and the two Houses of Parliament. Yet perhaps these facts are not conclusive. There are

1. W. C. Costin and J. S. Watson, *The Law and Working of the Constitution: Documents, 1660–1914* (1952), vol. 1, p. 7.

2. Amos J. Peaslee, *Constitutions of Nations*, vol. 3, pp. 544 ff.

certainly traditional statements which suggest that the nation is known to our jurisprudence. 'When Parliament acts,' wrote a sixteenth-century author, 'every Englishman is intended to be there present either in person or by procuration and attorneys.'[1] Statutes in this country do not have to be promulgated since they are assumed to be already known. Blackstone endorses the point: 'Every man is in judgment of law party to making an Act of Parliament.'[2] It is, in fact, only in rather recent times that constitutional commentators have been unanimous in excluding the people from their definitions of the formal source of sovereign authority in this country. In 1832 George Cornewall Lewis, in his *Remarks on the Use and Abuse of Some Political Terms*, protested that the use of the term 'sovereignty' to describe the universal participation of the people in electing representatives was 'improper' (though it appeared, he added, to be accepted in the United States of America). 'The right of voting for the election of one who is to possess a share of the sovereignty,' he wrote, 'is itself no more a share of the sovereignty than the right of publishing a political treatise or a political newspaper.'[3] But Lewis's editor in 1877 declared that his attribution of sovereignty to the legislature and his exclusion of the electorate had been 'definitely rejected by general usage'. John Austin, the nineteenth-century jurist, certainly regarded the possession and delegation of authority by the people to their representatives as a fact recognised by constitutional law. The supposition, he said, that the powers of the Commons are delegated entirely to the Commons' House probably arose from the fact that the terms of the trust are tacit rather than express, and that the sanctions are only moral ones. But 'speaking accurately, the members of the commons' house are merely trustees for the body by which they are appointed elected and . . . the sovereignty resides always in the King and the peers with *the electoral body of the commons*'.[4] Later writers have treated Austin's definition of the sovereign authority as an elementary confusion and adopted the distinction popularised by Dicey between 'legal sovereignty' exercised by the Queen-in-Parliament, and 'political sovereignty' exercised by the electorate. ('Electorate', 'People', and 'Nation', it should be noticed, cannot be used for this purpose entirely interchangeably, since the last two contain many persons who are not in fact electors). But Dicey's definitions are clumsy in implying that the distinction between the two sets of persons can be matched by the entirely different kind of distinction

1. Sir Thomas Smith, *De Republica Anglorum* (ed. Alston, 1906), pp. 48–9.
2. 1 *Commentaries*, 184.
3. 1877 ed., p. 44.
4. *The Province of Jurisprudence Determined*, Lecture VI, p. 230.

between the function of legislating and the function or right of exerting political influence to secure legislation. Clearly if the exercise of political sovereignty is the bringing to bear of non-legal power of influence it is not something which is confined to the electorate. Members of Parliament, as well as the Government and Civil Service collectively, are themselves part of the political sovereign as well as the electorate. Exercising political sovereignty is not what the electorate does as distinct from Parliament, but what everybody (including Parliament) does in his or their political capacity. Similarly legal sovereignty is not what Parliament has as distinct from the electorate, but what everybody (including the electorate) has in his or their legal capacity or status. But can it be argued that the electorate has a legal capacity? Austin at least, in including the electorate in his definition of the sovereign legal authority, was saying that it had, but that it had conferred the function of legislating upon its representatives; and there is no obvious reason why his description of the Constitution should be regarded as less apposite than Dicey's. He was not, after all, under any misapprehension as to the way in which legislation came about. It is conceded on this view that the people may not impress their will on a court of law directly, but must legislate through their representatives. As Sir Frederick Pollock remarked, an identical resolution passed by the electors of every constituency in England would have no legal force and no court of justice would be entitled to pay any attention to it.[1] But exactly the same is true in the United States or in India, whose constitutions explicitly declare that legislative institutions are founded upon the authority of the people. The claim does not of course imply either that the people legislate directly or that their assent is necessary to the validity of individual rules in a legal system. At least, therefore, it might be said that the British people is known to the law as having an elective function.

Dicey's distinctions tend to obscure this constitutional (as distinct from political, influential, or agitatory) role of the people. That legislators are the product of a specific legal process of election and not of any other process (e.g. self-appointment, nomination, or insurrection) is a fact which could hardly be omitted from any accurate account of the rules of our constitutional system. It is said that the office of Prime Minister is no longer entirely unknown to the law since several statutes now refer to it. A similar claim might be made on behalf of the People or the Nation. There must, after all, be some collectivity of the kind referred to by the Representation of the *People* Acts, or even (though more obliquely) to be inferred from the existence of such appellations as *British* Railways and the *National* Trust.

1. *A First Book of Jurisprudence* (5th ed.), p. 274.

3. *The characteristics of the Constitution*

The introductory chapters of works on the British Constitution make an interesting study. In the attempt to make plain the peculiar nature of the object they were about to describe successive writers in the nineteenth and early twentieth centuries coined a number of descriptive terms. On the whole they thought well of the Constitution. Hearn, in *The Government of England*, for example, wrote in 1868:

> While the mechanical contrivances of political inventors have crumbled away in the hands of the projectors, the goodly tree of British freedom selecting from the kindly soil and assimilating its fit nutriment still increases its stately bulk and still extends its unequalled development. Outliving the storms and vicissitudes of centuries, deeply rooted in the habits and affections of the people, it spreads far and wide its hospitable shade; and like the mustard tree in whose ever shading branches the fowls of the air find shelter it affords in the evil days to many a weary wing and many a scared and fluttering guest a secure asylum and an inviolable home.

In 1904 Sidney Low, in the opening chapter of his *Governance of England*, wrote:

> It is not so much that our constitution is unwritten, for of course much the largest part of it is written and printed, but that it is unfixed and flexible where others are rigid. We are not concerned with a solid building to which a room may be added here, or a wing there, but with a living organism in a condition of perpetual growth and change.

Four years later A. Lawrence Lowell remarked in similar vein that

> The system was not excogitated by an *a priori* method. . . . It has grown up by a continual series of adaptations. . . . In this it is like a living organism. There are no doubt many small anomalies and survivals that mar the unity for the purpose of description, but these like survivals of structure in animals, like the splint bones in the leg of a horse, for example, do not interfere seriously with the action of the whole.[1]

Reference to the Constitution as an organic growth, an 'edifice', an 'inheritance' and the like was always a popular device; but the metaphors conceal a number of different assertions. Sometimes, for example, the implication was merely that the Constitution, besides not being specifically labelled as such, is modified gradually rather than catastrophically. In addition (and rather differently) the suggestion was that it has no 'special' status, i.e. that no laws are immune from repeal by ordinary statute. 'Of all the characteristic features of the English Constitution . . .' wrote Sir John Marriot,

> there is none which strikes so oddly the imagination of foreign critics as the fact of perpetual and almost imperceptible modification. It was this

1. *The Government of England* (1908), vol. 1, p. 14.

which drew from Tocqueville the famous aphorism that in England 'there is no constitution'. On the lips of a Frenchman familiar with a long succession of written constitutions, each self-contained, each complete and coherent, the remark is not merely intelligible but obvious.[1]

The 'informality' or 'elasticity' or 'flexibility' of the Constitution is often linked with De Tocqueville's remark. 'Flexibility' as a term of art seems to have been introduced by Lord Bryce. In a lecture delivered in 1884 he contrasted 'flexible' constitutions which 'have elasticity because they can be bent and altered in form' with 'rigid' constitutions which 'cannot because their lines are hard and fixed'. The term 'flexible' has however been used in at least three different senses. It has been used to indicate the existence of, first, a *single process* for legislation; secondly, a *simple-majority* legislative process; and thirdly, a constitutional system in which it has as a matter of historical fact been fairly easy to make legal changes. A constitution which is 'inflexible' and 'difficult' to amend in the formal sense may have been amended without difficulty in fact. Conversely a constitutional system which is flexible in the sense of having a formally uncomplicated procedure for legal change may be one in which for political or social reasons fundamental changes are extremely difficult to bring about. The British Constitution is not obviously 'flexible' in this practical and historical sense at all. There is yet another use of the term 'flexible' which implies that rules of constitutional behaviour are not governed entirely by formal law and can be changed by informal means. Thus Sir Ivor Jennings speaks of the conventions of the Constitution ('the flesh which clothes the dry bones of the law'[2]) as an index of the flexibility of British institutions.

With such an amorphous object to describe, it is hardly surprising that constitutional reality flees before the commentator's pen. He may find himself dealing in 'maxims once true, but of which the truth is ceasing or has ceased', and he may (to use Bagehot's phrases still) be troubled by the difference between the living reality and the paper description. What is probably the earliest expression of the view that the formal parts of the Constitution function as a kind of façade occurs in William Paley's *Moral and Political Philosophy* published in 1785. 'In the British, and possibly in all other constitutions,' Paley wrote,

> there exists a wide difference between the actual state of the government and the theory. When we contemplate the theory of the British government, we see the King vested with . . . a power of rejecting laws. Yet when we turn our attention from the legal extent to the actual exercise of royal

1. *English Political Institutions* (1910), p. 26.
2. *The Law and the Constitution* (5th ed.), p. 81.

authority in England we see these formidable prerogatives dwindled into mere ceremonies; and in their stead a sure and commanding influence of which the constitution, it seems, is totally ignorant.[1]

The writer's difficulties might be classified under three heads. First, the difficulty of scope: What rules may properly be included in a description of the Constitution and what lie outside it? Secondly, the difficulty resulting from the opposition of theory and practice, or between legalistic fictions and the facts of political life; and thirdly the difficulty resulting from the existence of non-legal rules, which are regarded as binding (i.e. the 'conventions' of the Constitution).

4. *The scope of the Constitution*

It is not easy even to enumerate all the classes of statements which when set down could be called a fair description of the Constitution. To put a set of the Statutes of the Realm into the hands of an inquiring foreigner would hardly be a fair procedure, though it would not be to tell him lies about the British Constitution. Nor perhaps would he be much better informed after reading that the rights of the citizens of the United Kingdom to 'movement within, to, and from the Nation' are guaranteed by Magna Carta.[2] Certain ways of achieving realism by supplementing the formal outline are obvious. But lines would have to be drawn, in the first place, to prevent the realistic approach from becoming sociology. It is true, as Sir Ivor Jennings has observed, that 'A constitution in anything more than a formal sense is only an organisation of men and women. Its character depends upon the character of the people engaged in governing and being governed . . . and an examination of its working involves an examination of the social and political forces which make for changes in the ideas and desires and habits of the population and its various social strata.'[3] Clearly an examination of social forces in the community, however enlightening, is a much wider enterprise than anything which we normally think of as having 'constitutional' interest. In the second place a line has to be drawn to exclude the enumeration of every single rule determining the manner of exercise of governmental and public functions—many of which are better classified as administrative law or practice. On the other hand many rules which are not normally included perhaps ought to be—for example, certain decisions of Commonwealth courts and the International Court of Justice; or rules derived from International conventions and meetings

1. *Works* (Bohn's ed. 1856), p. 141.
2. Peaslee, *Constitutions of Nations*, vol. 3, p. 563. (Entry for UK in table headed 'Rights of the People'.)
3. *The Law and the Constitution*, p. 15.

of Commonwealth Prime Ministers. These are admittedly subject to the authority of, and alterable by, British statutes; but so are British judicial decisions and British conventions. Thirdly, a line of a different kind has to be drawn to distinguish statements which formulate rules, properly so-called, from statements which are merely generalisations, or comments. Here there may be a somewhat delicate distinction to be drawn between comments, inferences, and generalisations on the one hand, and conventions on the other. Fairly clear examples of generalisation are statements of the class, 'The United States Constitution is based on the Separation of Powers', 'Legislation in the United Kingdom is now as much a function of the executive as of the legislature'. These are not themselves statutory, judicial, or conventional rules—in fact they are not rules of any kind. At a fairly general level they might be called principles of the constitution. A typical enumeration of such principles for Britain would be 'Supremacy of Parliament', 'Cabinet Responsibility', 'Rule of Law'.[1] Often of course such statements are both descriptive generalisations and conventions. 'Cabinet Responsibility' is an example. It is both expository and prescriptive.

5. *Constitutional fictions*

The second type of descriptive difficulty, namely that arising from the opposition of formal theory and political practice, is sometimes expressed by saying that the British Constitution embodies 'fictions' which everybody knows to be untrue but to which, perhaps, for the sake of tradition and because they raise no practical obstacles to what anybody wants to do, lip service is periodically paid. A large part of the work of those who have written on the Constitution, wrote Sidney Low, has been to point out 'how the business of the nation gets itself done under cover of the historical fictions'. Some suggested fictions, however, may embody pretence, and some may not. Others may be true in certain senses and false in others. The legal omnipotence of Parliament, for example, is not exactly a 'pretence', though it is often called a legal 'fiction'. But it is no more and no less 'fictitious' than any other legal rule. It is not a fiction that Parliament might legally provide (to use a famous example) for the execution of all blue-eyed babies.[2] It is merely an unlikely political contingency—

1. W. Harrison, *The Government of Britain*, p. 26. cf. Dicey's three principles, the sovereignty of Parliament, the supremacy of the ordinary law of the land, and the dependence of the conventions upon the law.

2. Though possibly not Scottish babies, if it is true that 'the unlimited sovereignty of Parliament is a distinctively English principle, which has no counterpart in Scottish constitutional law'. (Lord Cooper, *obiter*, in *MacCormick v. Lord Advocate*, 1953, SC 396.)

though admittedly one which has been said to produce a conflict between academic logic and political reality.[1]

The word 'fiction' is perhaps most appropriate where there is a real conflict between an acknowledged practice and the general theory which is accepted as a respectable way of accounting for it and other practices. In 1953 a Select Committee of the Commons considered a proposal that certain divisions should not follow immediately upon the debate in the House but after an adjournment, during which it was said Members might read the debate in *Hansard.* Mr Herbert Morrison, opposing the proposal, said: 'I do not like blazoning out to the world that Parliament debates one night, and some night afterwards . . . it comes to a decision, because you are therefore shouting to the world that we are deliberately going to vote . . . on something which we know the bulk of us have not heard the merits of. If [he added] you once get away from the sequence of parliamentary debate, followed by a division, if any, the thing is unnatural . . . while it is perfectly true that the debate may proceed, and three-quarters of the Members taking part in the division may not have heard a word of it, nevertheless it is respectable on the face of it.'[2] Here the constitutional fiction may have a decisive effect in moulding feelings about action. Opposition to proposals to permit voting by proxy in the Commons may also, for example, be based upon a similar reluctance to countenance a procedure which makes plain what is true, namely that the purpose of divisions in the House is not primarily to reflect opinion about the merits of arguments used in the chamber. Perhaps this is not far removed from the sort of sham or falsehood with which Bentham and Dicey charged Blackstone. Yet such 'shams' may be in Great Britain, in some cases, all there is in place of a 'Founders' conception' of constitutional purposes and proprieties set out in a formal document. Formal theories of this kind are not impervious to changes in political practice, but there are points in the process of change at which they may become entangled with emerging conceptions and practices which carry different implications for action. Thus at the moment there exist potential disharmonies between a way of describing the Constitution which is not yet regarded as completely false or outdated, and a way of describing it which has not yet become quite acceptable or quite comfortable. Burke's description, for example, of the proper function of an elected representative is still in some sense orthodox, but it is an orthodoxy which parties, whips and pressure groups have subjected to a considerable strain. The same is true of

1. ibid.

2. *Select Committee on Delegated Legislation* (1953), HC 310, *Minutes of Evidence*, p. 81.

the idea of Parliament as a whole. It is still in some sense the case that Parliament is the 'grand inquest of the nation', that it decides the content of legislation, and that it controls the activities of the executive. Moreover, each of these statements may exert, and has exerted, a practical influence—for instance, on judicial decision when issues affecting the work of Parliament have arisen. Their influence, as we shall see, can be traced in judicial inferences and dicta about the 'intention of Parliament', and in cases involving parliamentary privilege. Yet each of these statements is in important respects false. The facts which they allege have become semi- if not whole-hearted fictions.

6. *Non-legal rules*

The third problem is that raised by the co-existence and interaction of law and convention in the Constitution. Political scientists since Dicey have devoted remarkably little time to conventions. They have adopted his description in its essentials and let the matter drop. Yet the chapters in which Dicey relates the conventions to the study of the Constitution form perhaps the least satisfactory part of his *Introduction.* Dicey himself, it may be remembered, was concerned to decide what as a constitutional lawyer he should be talking about. Certain classes of authors, he complained, led the student astray. Historians discussed the origins rather than the actuality of the Constitution. Lawyers, on the other hand, painted a picture of the Constitution which was simply false. 'We have all learnt from Blackstone and writers of the same class,' Dicey wrote, 'to make such constant use of expressions which we know not to be strictly true to fact, that we cannot say for certain what is the exact relation between the facts of constitutional government and the more or less artificial phraseology under which they are concealed.'[1] Perhaps oddly his next complaint was against political theorists (exemplified by Hearn and Bagehot), who described not the law of the Constitution but 'conventional understandings', 'constitutional morality', 'political ethics', and 'constitutional maxims'. These were not subjects with which a constitutional lawyer should concern himself at all. 'As a lawyer,' he said, 'I find these matters too high for me.'[2] Curiously enough he devoted the last part of the *Law of the Constitution* to a lucid discussion of matters which he professedly did not understand.

1. *Law of the Constitution* (10th ed.), p. 11.
2. op. cit., p. 21.

2

CONVENTIONS

1. *The meaning of 'conventions'*

There is an intimate relationship between the legal and non-legal rules of the Constitution. In the United States, the terms 'constitutional' and 'unconstitutional' are used to denote that a particular action is (or is not) in conformity with the fundamental law contained in the documentary constitution as it is interpreted and applied by the Supreme Court. In the United Kingdom, on the other hand, controversy rarely relates solely to the legal status of a disputed action. That the King had the *legal* right to refuse his assent to the Irish Home Rule Bill in 1913, for example, was agreed by all parties; but fierce argument continued about his *constitutional* right to do so. The point at issue then, as most commonly is the case, was the nature and extent of the powers permitted to the King by the non-legal rules of the Constitution. To those non-legal rules Dicey gave the name 'conventions', a terminology which is now generally followed in this country.

What then are the conventions of the British Constitution? One way of answering the question is to point to particular examples. Thus, among them are such rules as that the Monarch should normally, on the resignation of a government, ask the Leader of the Opposition to form the new one; or (before 1911) that the House of Lords should not oppose a money bill duly passed by the House of Commons; or (to quote from the Preamble to the Statute of Westminster of 1931) 'that any alteration in the law touching the Succession to the Throne or the Royal Style and Titles shall hereafter require the assent as well of the Parliaments of all the Dominions as of the Parliament of the United Kingdom'. An alternative approach is to put forward a formal definition. By the conventions of the Constitution, then, we mean certain rules of constitutional behaviour which are considered to be binding by and upon those who operate the

Constitution, but which are not enforced by the law courts (although the courts may recognise their existence), nor by the presiding officers in the Houses of Parliament. Not all writers would agree to the inclusion of this last phrase. But it seems best to exclude from the category of convention 'the law and custom of Parliament' which define much of its procedure, and which are applied and interpreted by, for example, the Speaker of the House of Commons. On the other hand, certain important rules of procedure—for example, resort to the usual channels through which, among other things, important decisions about the agenda of the House of Commons are reached—are 'unknown' both to the courts and to the Speaker and must clearly be counted as conventions.

Such conventions are to be found in all established constitutions, and soon develop even in the newest. One reason for this is that no general rule of law is self-applying, but must be applied according to the terms of additional rules. These additional rules may be concerned with the interpretation of the general rule, or with the exact circumstances in which it should apply, about either of which uncertainty may exist, and the greater the generality the greater will the uncertainty tend to be. Many constitutions include a large number of additional legal rules to clarify the meaning and application of their main provisions, but in a changing world it is rarely possible to eradicate or prevent all doubts on these points by enactment or even by adjudication. The result often is to leave a significant degree of discretion to those exercising the rights or wielding the powers legally conferred, defined, or permitted. As Dicey pointed out, it is to regulate the use of such discretionary power that conventions develop.[1] Thus the rules prescribing the procedure to be followed by the Monarch in the selection of a Prime Minister regulate the way in which she should exercise her prerogative power to appoint advisers. The legal prerogative remains intact, and appointments to the office of Prime Minister (itself a conventional position) can still be made only by the Monarch. Similarly, it remains true that no bill can become a statute until it receives the Royal Assent; but the Monarch's discretion in deciding whether or not to assent is governed by a rule that she should always assent to a bill which has duly passed both Houses. In this case the royal discretion is so limited as virtually to have been abolished. But the legal position remains untouched and thus, it is sometimes argued, may still be exercised under certain circumstances.

The definition of 'conventions' may thus be amplified by saying that their purpose is to define the use of constitutional discretion. To

1. ibid., pp. 426–9.

put this in slightly different words, it may be said that conventions are non-legal rules regulating the way in which legal rules shall be applied. Sometimes, of course, they do so only indirectly, in that they relate primarily to already existing conventions. Not all discretionary powers are so limited, but the most important ones usually are in some degree. In Britain it has been the growth of conventional limitations of the royal prerogative, in conjunction with changes in the legal rules contained in such statutes as the Act of Settlement and the various Acts extending the suffrage (as well as those changes brought about by judicial interpretation), which has largely created our modern system of government. As Sir Kenneth Wheare has said, it is 'the association of law with convention within the constitutional structure which is the essential characteristic'.[1] This is why it is impossible to settle constitutional disputes merely by reference to the state of the law.

Once having acknowledged the central role of conventions, the student of the British Constitution is liable to find that his troubles have only just begun. What exactly do these conventions say? How is he to find out what they say? Sometimes it is a simple matter. The principal conventions defining the relations between the various members of the Commonwealth, in so far as they were not translated into law by the Statute of Westminster, are to be found either in the Preamble to that Act, or in the Reports of the Imperial Conferences, or (since 1939) of the Conferences of Prime Ministers, at which they have been formally agreed upon and committed to writing. There also exists general agreement, although it is nowhere formally written down, that the Monarch should not ordinarily refuse her assent to legislation passed by Parliament. But what of other occasions? Would King George V have been acting constitutionally if he had 'vetoed' the Liberal Home Rule Bill?[2] Would he have been entitled to refuse to create a large body of new Peers in 1911, however necessary to secure the consent of the House of Lords to the Parliament Act of that year? Argument may also centre upon the question of whether any convention exists at all in certain areas of discretion. Sir Ivor Jennings has suggested, for example, that 'in framing social legislation the appropriate department must consult the appropriate "interest".'[3] The questions may legitimately be asked: Is this really a convention? And, if so, what exactly is the rule? Must every interest be consulted on every piece of social legislation? At what stage must

1. *The Statute of Westminster and Dominion Status* (5th ed.), p. 4.

2. See the arguments put forward by Dicey, printed and discussed in his *Law of the Constitution* (9th ed.), pp. 598–602.

3. *The Law and the Constitution* (5th ed.), pp. 102–3.

they be consulted? Must they be consulted only on social legislation? How does one set about answering questions of this kind?

2. *Conventions and usages*

It is sometimes said that there are two kinds of non-legal rule—conventions and usages. The most precise attempt to establish this distinction may be found in Sir Kenneth Wheare's valuable accounts of constitutional convention. 'By convention is meant an obligatory rule; by usage, a rule which is no more than the description of a usual practice and which has not yet obtained obligatory force.'[1] In consequence, 'it is often difficult to say whether a particular course of conduct is obligatory or persuasive only'.[2] There is, however, a difficulty in the commonsense distinction which is involved in saying that it is a convention that the Monarch should give her assent to any bill duly passed by both Houses of Parliament, but that her agreement to dissolve the House of Commons when requested to do so by the Prime Minister is a matter of usage, in that her consent is not mandatory under all circumstances. Not all authorities would agree that the first of these alone provides an example of an obligatory rule; but if the second may be assumed to be a 'usage', it could not with equal justice be referred to as a 'rule'. A rule must *prescribe* something if it is to guide action or state obligations, whereas, according to the definition here discussed, a usage would only describe actual behaviour. But the reasons why a particular action is not mandatory cannot lie in the fact that any statement about it is 'no more than description'. A description is not a weak kind of prescription. It is slightly odd to speak of a persuasive usage since usage is not a prescriptively tinged word at all. If a usage is to have any relevance to conduct it must be something like a rule to which the exceptions cannot easily be specified. Were the exceptions accurately specified, however (for example that the Monarch must grant a dissolution except under circumstances X, Y, and Z), the rule would be applicable in this form and would be a convention. The difficulties follow from picking out an *action* such as 'signing' or 'dissolving' and asking about its obligatoriness. But it is the *rule about dissolving* which is the convention. Correctly stated, it cannot fail to be obligatory.

On closer study, the 'usages' of the Constitution seem to refer to a variety of different things. Among them are: (1) Instances of

1. K. C. Wheare, *The Statute of Westminster and Dominion Status* (5th ed.), p. 10.

2. K. C. Wheare, *Modern Constitutions* (1951), p. 179—and see the whole discussion of the subject here.

general prescriptive rules (conventions) whose precise formulation is uncertain—for example the possible refusal by the Monarch to dissolve Parliament (the problem here is simply to formulate the conventional rule accurately); (2) Administrative practices which have been precisely formulated and written down—for example the methods of recruiting and grading Civil Servants (here, as has already been suggested, there is a problem of distinguishing such practices from the constitutional structure); (3) What might be called descriptive generalisations about governmental behaviour, including the normal responses of politicians to recurrent problems—for example the way in which the United States President, in appointing his Cabinet, 'will try to spread the appointments so that the main regions of the United States to which he attaches political importance will get some representation'.[1] (Generalisations of this type could hardly be omitted from any accurate account of a system of government and politics.)

It might perhaps be advisable to drop the term 'usage' altogether in the first of these senses. One advantage of so doing would be to avoid a difficulty relating to such a breach of convention as occurred when President Roosevelt was re-elected for a third term in 1940 in the face of an apparently well-established rule prohibiting it. Sir Kenneth Wheare has pointed out the oddity of this situation. 'Does it mean [he asked] that what appeared . . . in the United States up to 1940 to be a convention was in fact only a usage? Or is it more accurate to say that the convention existed up to that date and was amended or abolished, or even broken?'[2] One might perhaps say either that the rule had really been broken, or only that it had appeared to be. In the latter case, it would be matter for argument whether there had been acquiescence in a changed convention, or merely a distinction legitimately drawn within the original one—as a legal decision might be the result of reversing an earlier decision or of 'distinguishing' it.

The objection to be made against the convention-usage distinction is that when faced with a constitutional problem, it is appropriate to ask, first, which rules apply to the situation; secondly, what the precise content or meaning of these rules is; and thirdly, what significant facts about the situation may affect or determine application of the rule. To decide whether an action is governed by convention or 'usage' involves answering one or more of these questions, and the distinction itself provides only a slightly awkward way of classifying the answers when they are uncertain.

1. *Modern Constitutions*, p. 131, where this is referred to as a usage.
2. ibid., pp. 125–6.

If we return to Jennings's suggestion that a rule exists about consulting interests in the framing of social legislation, the objections may become clearer. In this instance it would be arguable that we are faced with a usage or set of usages. But is this an instance of a general (binding) rule about the obligation to govern by consent, or an accurate generalisation about administrative practice, or a true description of the normal political response, but not the only possible response, of British politicians? If it is agreed that some prescriptive rule applies, would it have been unconstitutional not to have consulted, say, the British Medical Association in establishing the National Health Service, or would only the complete absence of any outside consultation have been unconstitutional? These are the kinds of questions which need to be asked, and the convention-usage distinction offers no help.

3. *Establishing conventions*

The lack of formal adjudicative machinery in the sphere of non-legal rules means that it is difficult to decide questions about the formulation, application, and identification of conventions. Dicey does not face these difficulties directly, but his theory suggests a criterion for the third, namely that a number of accepted non-legal rules exist whose breach would lead to a clash with formal legal rules. The same criterion would also, perhaps, assist in their formulation and application. This is neat, but as has been pointed out by Jennings and others, it would at most apply to some of the conventions only. It offers neither a satisfactory account of the consequences of a breach, nor a satisfactory criterion for the settlement of disputes. However, as will be argued, Dicey was right to emphasise the need to attend to the *effects* of the conventions.

Sir Ivor Jennings's own account of conventions[1] is more convincing, but it is not entirely free from obscurity. His criteria for deciding whether a particular convention exists are these: 'First, what are the precedents; secondly, did the actors in the precedents believe that they were bound by a rule; and thirdly, is there a reason for the rule? A single precedent with a good reason may be enough to establish the rule. A whole string of precedents without such a reason will be of no avail, unless it is perfectly certain that the persons concerned regarded them as bound by it.'[2]

For a convention to exist and operate the actors must obviously be aware of it and, in particular, of its obligatory character (even if

1. In *The Law and the Constitution*, ch. III. Compare his *Cabinet Governments*, ch. I.
2. *The Law and the Constitution*, p. 136.

in fact they conform to it for reasons other than self-conscious virtue). This awareness of obligation is a necessary characteristic of a convention, but it is a sure guide only if this obligation is felt very generally among those who work the constitution, i.e. among the authorities. Its absence may be conclusive, but not its presence. In and of itself it is not and cannot be a sufficient test: the actors may be divided in their opinions or they may be mistaken about their obligations. Thus Jennings has argued[1] against the conclusive nature of King George V's appointment of Mr Baldwin in 1923 on the ground, in part, that even had the King thought himself bound to do so 'it might be that he was mistaken in thinking himself so bound'. (What exactly 'to be mistaken' means in this context needs discussion.) The test of awareness of 'obligation', in other words, cannot be invoked to settle any significant doubt or dispute, but at best only to demonstrate the existence of clearly established conventions when, by definition, there is no such dispute. But, of course, Jennings proposes that the test be used only in conjunction with those of 'precedent' and 'good reason'. It is not entirely clear, however, how the various tests are related to each other. Nor is it clear whether a 'good reason' here implies the making of an appraisal or the mere reporting of one. And if a single precedent with a good reason may establish a rule, there are some senses of the words 'reason' and 'establish' in which a single precedent with a *bad* reason may suffice to establish a rule. Since it is admittedly possible, furthermore, for a rule to be established by agreement, without any precedent, and, since a 'whole string of precedents' may not establish any rule, 'precedent' is clearly not conclusive. Again, Jennings suggests that a convention may arise solely on the basis of precedents in conjunction with a feeling of obligation, i.e. without a good reason, although he suggests that such a convention 'may be broken with impunity'.[2]

4. *Precedents*

How then are reasons for conventional rules related to precedents? In the English legal system all cases decided in the highest courts of the judicial hierarchy are precedents, in the sense that these decisions are binding upon all other courts in all other similar cases. In this manner, judicial decisions, or precedents, may be said to establish rules of law. (In subsequent cases the judges have, of course, to decide just what rule of law was established and whether it applies to the circumstances with which they are concerned.) In certain other legal systems, of which the Scottish is one example, it is said to be not

1. ibid., p. 136.
2. loc. cit.

the single precedent, but a stream of precedents, which establishes a rule of law. Where conventions are concerned, however, it seems that not even a series of similar precedent actions will always suffice to establish a conventional rule—if indeed it ever suffices. A distinction has therefore been drawn by Sir Ivor Jennings between precedents which do, and those which do not, establish a rule, i.e. between 'normative' and 'simple' precedents.[1] But both in legal and ordinary English we tend to use the word 'precedent' to refer to instances which, for some reason other than the fact of occurrence itself, are deemed to be relevant, desirable, or acceptable models for future action. (Sir Ivor remarks at one point the 'agreement to differ' amongst Ministers in 1932, 'No harm was done by the precedent of 1932 provided that it is not regarded as a precedent.'[2]) A 'simple' precedent, in other words, could hardly be distinguished from no precedent at all. Like convention, 'precedent' has a prescriptive flavour. 'Simple precedents' could well go into limbo along with 'usages'.

The instance of 1923 is an instructive one. It is justifiable to query the opinion that King George V established a new rule (that the Prime Minister should always be a Member of the House of Commons) when he appointed Mr Baldwin instead of Lord Curzon. On the other hand, there now seems to exist a widespread view that a Prime Minister should not belong to a Chamber in which one party has little representation and in which few major debates or decisions occur. For some such reason, the King's action of 1923 may now be referred to as a precedent. But this reason would have existed whether or not there had existed a noble alternative to Mr Baldwin. Not even to the Common Lawyer will every previous instance constitute a 'precedent'. Nevertheless, a previous instance may be persuasive for many reasons. At the lowest level, the mere fact that something has been done before may comfort the cautious (which is probably the nearest thing one finds to a 'simple' precedent), but this is persuasive only as against the completely novel. Precedents certainly may be a helpful guide in so far as they provide suggestions for the formulation of a rule. But even as such their use is limited. Disagreement will often continue to exist about the precise content of the rule for which precedents provide the evidence. Disagreement may also exist about the precise circumstances in which a rule applies. Moreover conditions change, and with them the rules. Thus Jennings has pointed out that 'precedents arising before 1832 must be used in rare cases

1. Jennings's *Cabinet Government* (2nd ed.), p. 7. The distinction, but not the labels, are retained in the 3rd ed., p. 6.

2. ibid. (3rd ed.), p. 281.

only, for the Reform Act altered the fundamental assumption of the Constitution'[1] and Mackintosh suggests that 'the principles underlying contemporary politics only really began to operate after the Reform Act of 1867 had its effect'.[2] But the changes in circumstances need not be either so drastic or so specific as those produced by the Reform Acts for them to be relevant and sometimes conclusive.

5. *Obedience to conventions*

Neither a general feeling of obligation among the authorities, nor precedents, therefore, suffice either to establish a rule or conclusively to demonstrate its existence and precise content. On the other hand, particularly in a society in which tradition is as venerated as it is in Britain, both these tests have an important part to play. But it is necessary, in case of dispute, always to appeal to the principles involved in a situation, in order to assess the weight of authority and precedent or to evaluate a novel situation.

About the general purpose of these principles, both Dicey and Jennings are agreed. For the former, conventions secure 'what is called abroad the sovereignty of the people'; for the latter the conventions exist because 'they are consistent with and are implied in the principles of the Constitution. Of these, there are four of major importance. The British Constitution is democratic; it is parliamentary; it is monarchical; and it is a cabinet system.'[3] These statements command general assent today, as would probably the further statement that the conventions should be interpreted and applied in order to further the ends listed. But these principles, helpful though they may be, are as much generalisations from constitutional behaviour as they are reasons for it, and they have been neither constant nor always agreed upon. Furthermore, if one accepts Jennings's fuller list rather than Dicey's, problems of 'priority' present themselves. For example it is not difficult to envisage a conflict between certain ideas of monarchy and of democracy. One must ask, therefore, how and why the principles come to be recognised, which is to ask why conventions come into existence and are obeyed.

The first part of the answer is contained in Jennings's suggestion that 'conventions are obeyed because of the political difficulties which follow if they are not'.[4] To complete the answer one must

1. ibid., p. 8.

2. J. P. Mackintosh, *The British Cabinet* (1962), p. 18. See also the discussion of the effects of the party system on the rules at p. 44 below.

3. In, respectively, *The Law of the Constitution* (10th ed.), p. 431, and *Cabinet Government* (3rd ed.), p. 13. For some purposes it may be argued that these principles should themselves be considered as conventions.

4. *The Law and the Constitution*, p. 34.

inquire what sort of political difficulties they are, for it is clear that political difficulties can arise from many actions which involve no breach of a convention. A government runs into 'political difficulties' whenever it displeases some section of the community, whether it be by raising rents or refusing to issue a stamp commemorating the birth of Robert Burns, but it cannot seriously be claimed that either decision is in any sense 'unconstitutional'. Nevertheless it is by examining the effects of a breach of conventions that the reason for their existence is to be found. If a United Kingdom Government had, before 1931, legislated for a 'Dominion', or had, since then, introduced legislation affecting the status of the Crown, without obtaining the consent of the countries concerned, it is likely that one or more members of the Commonwealth might have severed their connections with it; or, at least, that Commonwealth ties would have been imperilled. The serious breach in the conventions limiting the power of the House of Lords which occurred in 1909 resulted directly in the passing of the Parliament Act of 1911, just as Roosevelt's re-election for a third and fourth term led to the adoption of the 22nd Amendment to the American Constitution which makes a third term legally impermissible. If one takes the example of the conventions limiting the powers of the Monarch it can similarly be argued that a breach would endanger the status or even the existence of the Monarchy.[1] These examples indicate that the conventions describe the way in which certain legal powers must be exercised if the powers are to be tolerated by those affected. The Monarch's legal powers to rule, the House of Lords' legal powers to reject a bill passed by the Commons, the legal power of the United Kingdom Parliament to pass imperial legislation—all these powers are or were retained only for so long as they are exercised (or not exercised) in accordance with the conventions which have been established. Their potential abolition constitutes the 'political difficulties' which would probably follow upon a breach in the conventions of the Constitution.

From this view of the nature of conventions it follows that the crucial questions must always be whether or not a particular class of action is likely to destroy respect for the established distribution of authority and whether or not it is likely to maintain respect for the constitutional system of changing (or sustaining) the distribution of authority.

Such an account of the relationship between law and convention bears a resemblance to that put forward by Dicey, but it differs therefrom in an important respect. According to Dicey a breach in a

1. cf. G. C. Moodie, 'The Crown and Parliament', X *Parliamentary Affairs*, 3, pp. 256–64; and ch. 3 below.

convention involved the probability of a consequential breach of the law. But the truth is rather that a breach of a convention is likely to induce a change in the law, or even in the whole constitutional structure. In this relationship, it may be suggested, is to be found the 'reason' for the conventions, stated in its most general form. In any given situation other, more specific, reasons may be immediately apparent—for example, the requirements of smooth and efficient administration, the prevailing beliefs about the nature of good government, or the demands of some powerful social group. But these reasons give rise to conventions rather than, say, administrative practices, only if to ignore them is seriously to endanger the legal *status quo*. The third criterion, that of 'reason', is therefore the critical one in the case of fundamental disputes about the conventions (in which disputes it is often particularly difficult to separate arguments about what the rules are from ones about what the rules ought to be). It is not possible, however, nor is it desirable, simply to dispense with the other criteria. Reference to precedents, for example, may be useful because they indicate what has been 'got away with' in the past, or what was believed to be undesirable even to attempt, or what, under the circumstances, had to be done. A previous instance becomes a precedent because it demonstrates these things. An action with undesirable consequences (even if the consequences were not considered undesirable at the time) may for these reasons be considered a bad precedent. On the other hand, since the political consequences of an action inevitably depend upon the precise circumstances, and particularly upon such things as the prevailing political beliefs, the distribution of power in society, and the nature and urgency of the political problems facing the Government, it follows that precedents of themselves can never provide conclusive justification for the continuing existence of a general rule. The authoritative convictions of those who work the Constitution derive force not only from the fact that a rule cannot be said clearly to exist unless it is recognised by those whom it purports to bind, but also from the fact that the leading actors are peculiarly well placed to know what political circumstances in fact require. By the same token, it becomes possible to attach an intelligible meaning to the notion that the authorities may be mistaken in their beliefs, for even they may make a wrong assessment of the situation and its potentialities. The appeal to the principles of the Constitution also, under most circumstances, retains its validity. The concept of constitutional principles is admittedly capable of several interpretations: it may mean the basic assumptions and ideals of those who work the Constitution; broad generalisations about the general character of the Constitution derived from observation of its working; or simply what those making the appeal believe the general character is or ought to be. During times of relative stability these alternative interpretations will tend to coincide and thus provide a useful signpost. At other times the appeal to 'principle' will be no more than an *ex parte* weapon used in constitutional debate.

6. *The enactment of conventions*

Dr H. V. Evatt has argued that the practice of enacting conventions, exemplified in such laws as the Parliament Act and the Statute of Westminster, should be extended into other fields in order to end uncertainty about, for example, the royal power of dissolution.[1] In so far as this would lead to more precise formulation of the rules and the use of the courts to give authoritative decisions about their meaning and application, or to the extent that people are more disposed to obey legal than non-legal rules, the advantages are obvious and important. It is nevertheless argued by some that the disadvantages are of greater significance. Thus the Statute of Westminster was resisted in the House of Lords on the grounds that this country 'never has had a written constitution of any sort or kind, and the consequence has been that it has been possible to adapt, from time to time, the various relationships and authorities between every component part of this State, and without any serious mistake or disaster. . . . You should avoid as far as possible putting a definition of what the relationships may be into the unyielding form of an Act of Parliament.'[2] This view is hard to accept. Quite apart from the fact that statutes may be repealed or amended with relative ease by a determined government, or that what are conventions in one country may exist as laws elsewhere without any disastrous effects, the objection overlooks the fact that new conventions may come to qualify any legal rule. British constitutional history would have been very different were statute-law necessarily a source of 'disastrous rigidity' in the Constitution.

It would be equally wrong, however, to over-estimate what enactment of the conventions would achieve. Let us try to draw up a 'balance sheet' of what it could and could not do. (1) Obedience to the rules would not become any more enforceable than it is now. There would undoubtedly be occasions when the mere clarification of a rule would ensure constitutional behaviour. The courts, more-

1. *The King and his Dominion Governors*. See, in particular, his list of difficult points at p. 268.

2. Lord Buckmaster, quoted in Wheare: *The Statute of Westminster and Dominion Status*, pp. 5–6, where the argument is rejected.

over, can do much to secure observance of the law by such means as declarations and injunctions. But there are severe limits to the effectiveness of judicial, or even legislative, action in the face of determined opposition to the law by a government, or for that matter, by any powerful social group. The sanctions behind constitutional law, as well as convention, are a compound of the desire to abide by the rules, to be 'constitutional', and of the political penalties of disobedience. Ultimately, revolution or civil war may be necessary to procure obedience, as has been amply demonstrated by the history of American legislation and adjudication upon the rights of the Negro population in the South; (2) In the absence of a sufficient body of judicial decisions even well-established legal principles may (at any given time) be of uncertain formulation and application: the principle of the Sovereignty of Parliament itself is a case in point. However, in the event of an important dispute turning upon the interpretation of a legal rule, the machinery exists for an authoritative decision upon its meaning and precise application; (3) Legislation, as we have noted, would not prevent the growth of new conventions, about which uncertainty may exist; (4) It could not prevent dispute about what the rules ought to be. And it is important to realise that it is this type of dispute which underlies many arguments about (apparently) what the rules are. This was obviously the case, for example, in the argument about the royal power to 'veto' legislation which took place in 1913, or the Commons' debates about the extent of parliamentary privilege in 1958. It would be foolish to expect anything else, for convention may be described as the 'battleground' between conflicting political forces and constitutional beliefs in society. But this is true not only of disputes about conventional rules. It applies also to legal argument. To cite American experience again, it is evident that constitutional debates about racial segregation in education, or the powers of the Federal Government in the social and economic fields, have been more than mere scholarly disputations about the 'real' meaning of the 14th Amendment or the 'inter-state commerce clause', although this is the way in which they may be presented. Primarily, these debates have been attempts to persuade the Supreme Court Justices of what the documentary constitution ought to mean; and the standing of the court at any period will depend, in part, upon whether its interpretations conflict with the wishes and beliefs of the most powerful forces in society at the time .Conversely, it is at least arguable that the high standing of the British courts owes something to the fact that many of the most important constitutional rules are, at present, of a non-legal character. Another important factor is, of course, that the doctrine of parliamentary supremacy saves the

British courts from having to give the last word on legal points. However, it is doubtful whether this would prevent the courts from a loss of prestige if they were constantly called upon to decide (even subject to parliamentary 'reversal') a whole series of constitutional controversies; (5) What has just been said suggests that the attempt to enact conventional rules might itself prove extremely difficult. It is likely that the fiercely disputed Parliament Act of 1911 rather than the Statute of Westminster would prove to be typical of the process. Even if agreement could be reached about what the rules are, it is hard to believe that no attempt would be made to formulate the rule with greater precision, in line with particular views as to what it should be. It can be argued, with some conviction, that this is in fact what happened with the Parliament Act and with the American 'third-term' amendment.[1] It is, moreover, most unlikely that in fact any attempt will be made to 'codify' the conventions until and unless their precise meaning has become a crucial factor in a constitutional crisis—in which case it might not be of very great significance whether the disputed rule was or was not a law, in that further legislation may anyway be needed to settle the dispute; (6) Enactment of the conventions may nevertheless be important, if once successfully achieved. Just as some course of action desired by a section of the community acquires a significant degree of legitimacy and authority simply in virtue of its acceptance as a convention, so a convention may acquire greater legitimacy and authority by its transformation into law. The exact significance of this 'elevation' will probably vary with different rules; (7) Enactment would be of greatest importance, perhaps, in the context which Dr Evatt seems to have had principally in mind, namely the 'export' of the British Constitution to other countries. In setting up new constitutional structures it may well be desirable that the most vital rules be formulated with the greater precision normally associated with the law. Even so, there is no reason to think that a more precise formulation of the rules would have enabled any of Britain's formerly dependent territories to avoid the constitutional disturbances with which many of them have been plagued.

1. To this extent, perhaps some force should be allowed to the objection made by Lord Buckmaster, however misplaced one might believe it to have been in the case of the Statute of Westminster whose principal effect, after all, was to remove legal hindrances to the full operation of the established conventions.

3

THE CROWN

1. *Conventional responsibility*

In law, Ministers are like other royal servants. They are appointed by the Monarch, may be dismissed by the Monarch, and are thus presumably responsible to the Monarch for their conduct. But this is true only in law. Constitutionally the relationship between Monarch and Ministers is regulated by the conventional doctrine of ministerial responsibility. By this phrase is meant (briefly) that Ministers are responsible *for* the general conduct of government, including the exercise of many powers legally vested in the Monarch; and that they are responsible *to* Parliament immediately, and ultimately, through Parliament and parties, to the electorate. When the British system of government is described as one of responsible government, it is to the doctrine of ministerial responsibility that reference is primarily being made. Given its fundamental place in the modern constitution, it is all the more noteworthy that there should exist uncertainty as to its precise extent and application. In this and the following chapters some of the uncertainties will be explored, beginning here with that aspect which concerns the relations between Ministers and the Monarch.

About the ordinary everyday constitutional powers of the Monarch there is no dispute: the Queen exercises her formidable legal powers only upon the advice of a responsible Minister or Ministers, and may not reject the advice they give. Politically she must be impartial in public, and discreet in private. She may attempt to influence the conduct of government, but the decisions are taken by Her Majesty's Government, severally or collectively. In our constitutional monarchy, as in others in Europe, the basic principle is that normally the Monarch does not govern, but must subordinate herself, in her political activities, to those who do, her official advisers. By this separation of legal and conventional responsibility it has been possible to maintain intact the legal structure of hereditary Monarchy within a democratic form of government. Only thus could the Monarchy have survived into an age when hereditary status no longer carried with it the authority to rule, and when the powerful sections of the community insisted that the government be responsible to them. This demand could not be met by the Monarchy: being hereditary and not elective it could not easily become politically accountable to the governed, while the doctrine that *rex non potest peccare* stood in the way of any developing alternative of legal accountability. The Monarchy had no real option, therefore, but progressively to relinquish its governmental powers. (These comments, it should be added, are intended to be analytical rather than historical in character, and to indicate logical rather than historic connections. The actual development of the modern doctrine of ministerial responsibility was much more involved and much less purposive than these comments would suggest.)

The word 'responsible' has several meanings in the constitutional context, which must be noted. The difference between legal and conventional responsibility is rarely overlooked. Within the second of these categories, however, a further distinction may be made between mere accountability, as it may be called, and moral responsibility (culpability). To say that someone is responsible (in the sense of accountable) may sometimes be to say that he is the proper person to be visited with the constitutional consequences of an action, or that he is the person under whose authority the action was taken. On the other hand to say that he is responsible (in the second sense) may be to imply that he is either the actual agent, or the person morally deserving blame or praise for the action.[1]

'Culpability' might be reserved for the second of these notions and 'accountability' for the first were it not that 'culpability' suggests blame exclusively. As it happens, however, questions of responsibility tend to be raised and constitutional disputes tend to be prompted by actions of which people in fact *dis*approve. 'Accountability' is open to a different kind of objection when applied, for example, to certain actions of the Monarch. The word implies the existence of some constitutional means of holding a person to account, of making him render account. Ministers are ultimately accountable in that they may be forced to resign or fail to be re-elected; but the very essence of the Monarch's position is that there exists no comparable constitutional machinery.

In so far as the penalties exacted of the accountable person tend to vary with the degree of his culpability, there is a tendency for the two types of responsibility to coincide, or for those concerned to seek

1. cf. ch. 4 below, particularly at pp. 52–4.

the means of bringing them together. It is possible, indeed, to see the development of ministerial responsibility as an example of this process, with Ministers seeking to become culpable as well as in part accountable for royal acts of government, and succeeding when once the party system has provided them with an alternative basis for their power and position. There is a point beyond which men will not shield others, and after which they will insist that they be responsible (accountable) only for their own actions.

2. *The 'personal' prerogatives*

Today the powers of the Crown (the prerogatives) have largely been transferred to elected Ministers who are responsible in both senses for their exercise. But not entirely so: there continue to exist personal prerogatives for which, under certain circumstances, the Monarch is said by some writers to be personally responsible. These powers include certain relatively minor ones, like the conferment of some Honours or, less minor, the appointment of the Queen's Private Secretary, as well as major ones pertaining to the selection of a Prime Minister, the dissolution of Parliament, the dismissal of a government, and the refusal of the Royal Assent to a bill passed by Parliament. Only the major ones have given rise to serious constitutional problems. We will therefore confine our attention to them.

The Monarch's powers in relation to the dissolution of Parliament, the dismissal of Ministers, and the giving of assent to bills may conveniently be treated separately from the selection of a Prime Minister, which involves a different kind of 'exception' to the doctrine of ministerial responsibility. The selection of a Prime Minister patently cannot be subject to the normal machinery for ministerial responsibility, as we shall see. In this respect it is unique among the Monarch's powers. The other powers under consideration are, arguably at least, subject to that machinery. The problem about them is to decide whether there exist any circumstances under which the Monarch may constitutionally use her discretion in exercising the powers of dismissal, dissolution, or assent.

3. *Dissolution, dismissal, and assent*

In 1913 a section of the Unionist Party urged the King to 'veto' the Home Rule Bill. Had the King done so, it would have been the first use of this prerogative since the reign of Queen Anne, whereas instances of the others can be cited from the nineteenth century. Partly for this reason, not even an ardent Unionist like Dicey seemed prepared to countenance this proposal. But he did lend support to the view that the King was entitled to insist upon the holding of an early dissolution (even at the cost of forcing the resignation of the Liberal Government) in order to test public opinion. As he pointed out in a letter to *The Times*, this would or could accomplish all that was claimed for the 'veto'.[1] Any refusal to give Royal Assent to a measure passed by Parliament would in fact inevitably raise questions about the prerogatives of dissolution and dismissal.

Walter Bagehot, in his *English Constitution*, argued strongly that it was undesirable, for the sake of good government, that the Monarch should be vested with these powers.[2] His arguments have not prevented the continuation of controversy. Nor, apparently, have authority or precedent provided conclusive evidence about the rules which regulate the use of these crucial powers. It is significant, for example, that substantially similar ground was covered by the correspondents on this subject in *The Times* in September 1913, and in April 1950. Roughly speaking there are two lines of argument, the divergence between which is, at first sight, remarkably small. There appears to be universal agreement that the Monarch may never use these powers arbitrarily and entirely on his own responsibility: some Ministers must be prepared to advise and then defend the Monarch's action. But whereas one view implies that a Monarch may actively seek Ministers who are prepared to give the desired advice, the other insists that a Monarch is restricted to accepting the advice of whichever Ministers are in office at the time (or, in other words, that these are not personal prerogatives at all). Neither of these positions is entirely free from objection. Before discussing them, however, it would be useful to look briefly at the precedents to which reference is sometimes made.

In the United Kingdom no Monarch has refused a dissolution when requested by a Prime Minister, or forced one against advice; nor has a government been dismissed (unless one counts Peel's resignation over the 'bedchamber question' in 1839) since Queen Victoria came to the throne. Examples from earlier periods are numerous, but it is doubtful how far they can properly be regarded as precedents for the very changed circumstances of today. For more recent precedents one must turn to other parts of the Commonwealth with similar constitutions. The Governor-General of Canada in 1926 and the Governor-General of South Africa in 1939, wielding the powers of the Crown, refused a dissolution to the then Prime Minister. In each case, therefore, he had no option but to resign. In each case an alternative Government was available—the Canadian one lasting only a

1. 15 September 1913. This and other contributions to the controversy are quoted in Jennings, *Cabinet Government*, app. III.

2. W. Bagehot, *The English Constitution* (1867), ch. VII.

few days before being forced itself to request a dissolution (which was granted), and the South African one maintaining a majority until after the war had been won. In each case, too, the Governor-General became the target of criticism coming mainly from supporters of the government which had, in effect, been dismissed. Even were it universally agreed that the Governors-General had acted constitutionally, which it is not, one could not safely conclude that the same judgment would apply to similar action by a Monarch in the United Kingdom (or elsewhere). It is not certain, for one thing, that precisely the same rules must always apply in the United Kingdom as in the other Commonwealth countries whose constitutions derive from it. More important, it is not certain that the same rules apply to a Governor-General as to the Sovereign in person. Admittedly the powers of a Governor-General are officially the same as those of the Monarch in the United Kingdom but, in the absence of any clear formulation of the latter, it is not easy precisely to enumerate those powers. It cannot be disputed that in 1926 and 1939 the Governors-General exercised powers which had once belonged to the Monarch. Furthermore, had these actions been taken by the Monarch personally, and been accepted as constitutional at the time, it could not be disputed that they were instances of powers properly belonging to Governors-General. That is to say that what the Queen may do, her representatives may do also, in the absence of any legal provision to the contrary. But it does not necessarily follow that what is done by them may constitutionally be done by the Queen. The essential point to remember is that a Governor-General is, nowadays, appointed for a limited term on the advice of the Commonwealth government concerned, and thereafter acts on the advice of Commonwealth Ministers, and not on the advice or instruction either of Ministers or of the Monarch in the United Kingdom. It follows that his involvement in controversy concerns himself alone, and not necessarily the place of the Crown. The temporary and appointive nature of his office, moreover, means that the real or apparent partisanship of any one incumbent need imperil nothing more than his own tenure. Neither of these statements can safely be made about the Monarch personally. It must be concluded, therefore, that these precedents provide no clearer guidance than do the opinions of constitutional authorities.

Amongst these opinions what might be called the 'older' doctrine (in the sense of having been advocated for the longer time, and not necessarily in the sense of being old-fashioned or out of date) was put clearly by Sir William Anson in his letter to *The Times* (10 September 1913) in which he said that 'if the King should determine, in the interests of the people, to take a course which his Ministers disapprove, he must either convert his Ministers to his point of view, or, before taking action, must find other Ministers who agree with him'. Mr Asquith in 1923, and Mr Churchill in 1944, expressed similar views about the right to *refuse* a request for a dissolution, and other authorities could also be quoted to the same effect.[1] Despite the existence of many *prima facie* precedents which might seem to support this argument, important grounds of principle have been advanced against it by proponents of the 'newer' doctrine, labelled the 'automatic' doctrine by Lord Hugh Cecil in his contribution to *The Times* correspondence of 1913. Leaving aside the vital question of how the King shall determine what is 'in the interests of the people', the essential objection to an exercise of the power to refuse or insist upon a dissolution is the difficulty thereafter of keeping the Monarch out of politics, particularly under a two-party system, however strenuous the efforts of his new Ministers to shoulder the responsibility. The other party, and possibly a majority of the electorate, would still hold the Monarch culpable—and rightly so. *The Times*' leading article of 8 September 1913 put the objection thus: 'A dissolution of Parliament by an exercise of the Royal Prerogative, *proprio motu regis*, might be followed by a vindication at the polls of those very Ministers whose advice had been set aside', thereby producing a situation where the Monarch is in open disagreement with his people. Even if this did not happen, the fact is that *beforehand* there is no certainty that it will not. More is required to protect the Monarch's position than the probability of an electoral majority in support of his policy. As Lord Chorley has put it: 'It is very important that in such circumstances the King should be bound by a clear and simple rule which there can be no mistaking, and this is exactly what the convention that he must accept the advice of his Prime Minister provides.'[2] The 'old' rule satisfies this requirement, of course, in the sense that it is capable of a clear and simple formulation. On the other hand, it does not prescribe any one simple line of action to be followed by the Monarch. In order to discover whether alternative advice is obtainable the Monarch may become involved in complicated and protracted negotiations with political leaders. To distinguish justifiable consultation from improper intrigue may then prove very difficult. To this extent the 'old' rule is probably not sufficiently clear and simple.

Two other objections may be quoted. Mr Roy Jenkins pointed out in 1950 that if Mr Attlee were refused a dissolution, Mr Churchill (as the only alternative Prime Minister) would have to be granted one,

1. See Lord Simon's letter to *The Times*, 24 April 1950. None now argue that the Crown may *force* a dissolution.
2. *The Times*, 26 April 1950.

'and the Crown would be placed in the intolerable and dangerous position of granting to a minority Prime Minister what it had recently refused to a majority Prime Minister'.[1] The King would thus necessarily have appeared to favour one of the two major political parties. The other objection was put forward by Professor J. H. Morgan in the earlier *Times* correspondence. 'The right of dissolution,' he wrote, 'regarded as a ministerial right, owes its existence to a general recognition of the Sovereign's immunity from responsibility for its exercise; until that immunity was achieved any dissolution was a source of grave anxiety to the Sovereign as carrying with it the implication that not only was the Ministry defeated, but the Crown compromised or, to use the language of Queen Victoria in the early days of her reign, "affronted".' Here one can see not only a convincing argument against the 'old' theory, but also the reason why it should perhaps be superseded. In present times the Monarch is expected to refrain from political intervention to an extent unknown a century and more ago. What was accepted as legitimate political influence then is not so accepted now when a greater emphasis is placed on such conceptions as 'the sovereignty of the people'. Whether in fact people would vote for or against a government which was believed to possess royal support, it is now generally felt to be undesirable that this be an issue at all. Governments and parties should be supported or opposed on their merits and their record, and not on their acceptability to the Monarch. Only if a dissolution is felt to be the decision of the Prime Minister, not of the Monarch, can an election be freed from the essentially irrelevant question of royal preferences. And only thus may the Monarch satisfy the constitutional requirement that she be, in fact and appearance, politically impartial.

If these considerations are conclusive there appears to be no issue which could justify refusal of a dissolution in a two-party system. Similar arguments apply *a fortiori* against the dismissal of a government. But does it follow that one must accept a complete 'automatic' theory? There is one situation in which such a theory should not probably be acted upon. If a Prime Minister has been defeated at a general election and then requests another immediate dissolution, the Monarch would surely be entitled, if not obliged, to refuse the request, always assuming that an alternative government could be formed without another election. The doctrine of ministerial responsibility is designed not only to safeguard the Monarchy from political involvement, but also to ensure that the power to govern is wielded by those who have the authority to govern. This authority can hardly be claimed by a Prime Minister who has been clearly

1. ibid.

rejected by the electors in favour of another man or party. For the Monarch to refuse him a second immediate dissolution would therefore be to uphold the authority of the electorate against an attempt to undermine the whole constitutional system. Of course, if the electoral verdict is confused, in the sense that no other government can be formed either, then on either theory the Monarch ought to accede to the request and allow the electorate the opportunity to make a fresh decision. Even if the electoral verdict is clear the Monarch may still prefer to leave it to the electorate to penalise the Prime Minister who has challenged that verdict. The essential point is that to grant or withhold a dissolution would probably, under the circumstances envisaged, be a matter for the Monarch's discretion. The principle seems to be clear, although it is possible to imagine a situation in which its application would not be. It is difficult, for example, to decide in advance whether the rule applies on the basis of upholding the authority of the electorate when a Prime Minister, who has lost his parliamentary majority, has yet obtained (say) 60 per cent of the votes cast; or when the request for a second dissolution is made not within a few days of Parliament's assembly but, possibly because of a small shift in parliamentary allegiance, after one or even two months.

A major source of difficulty and confusion is that the behaviour constitutionally demanded of the Monarch may differ according to the number and nature of the political parties with which she is confronted. At least some of the gap between proponents of the 'old' and 'new' doctrines of ministerial responsibility may be explained by the fact that the 'new' one pertains most clearly to the modern two-party system, while the 'old' draws largely upon experience of a time when parties were more numerous or less coherent, and pertains rather to a minority government's relations with the Crown. To dismiss the Government, or dissolve Parliament against its wishes, may be considered undesirable in any circumstances, but it may be that it is only under a disciplined two-party system that the right to *refuse* a dissolution should be as restricted as the 'new' rule implies. Whether the problem is one of the content of the relevant rules, or of their application, is a matter for debate. The party system is also an important, and complicating, factor in relation to the other personal prerogatives to be discussed here.

4. *Selection of a Prime Minister*

The most frequently invoked of the so-called personal prerogatives is the selection of a Prime Minister. It has already been noted that the constitutional problem here is to discover and state what rules apply, given that no *Minister* can be responsible in the ordinary way for the Monarch's decision. On this last point there is general agreement. Clearly there could be no 'automatic' theory which made the advice of the outgoing Prime Minister or Cabinet mandatory as to the person who should be invited to form a new government. The objections to this procedure are threefold. It must be remembered, firstly, that ministerial responsibility involves the principle that a Minister be accountable or answerable to Parliament for his actions, the ultimate sanction being the loss of his office. But in the instance given, this sanction would not apply: since he was retiring from office in any case, the possibility of losing the confidence of Parliament or electorate would hold no terrors for him. He would be culpable but not fully accountable, the very disjunction of responsibilities which the system of ministerial responsibility is designed normally to prevent. The second objection is that a defeated Prime Minister, as distinct from one who voluntarily resigns in favour of another member of his own party, is clearly without the parliamentary authority to give mandatory advice. The third is that for a retiring Prime Minister to have the right to nominate his successor is to grant him a potentially important power without the assurance that it would not be used in a highly partisan or even capricious way. This is most obvious with reference to a two-party system. One has only to imagine what might have happened had a mischievous Conservative selected Mr Bevan in 1945, or an impish Labour Leader chosen Mr Butler in 1951, to see how anomalous the power would be. The point of these examples, it should be said, is not that Mr Bevan and Mr Butler would necessarily have been worse Prime Ministers than the men actually selected, but that their selection (assuming that they would have accepted office) would have imposed a possibly fatal strain upon the unity of their parties at the time. It may be argued that no person likely to become Prime Minister would ever behave in so untrustworthy a fashion, but of this there can be no certainty.

It is in fact generally accepted that the Monarch is not bound to accept ministerial advice in her selection of a Prime Minister. For the use of this power she is personally culpable. But it is sometimes argued that she is not constitutionally accountable, and that all responsibility (in this sense) lies with the incoming Prime Minister. This was the view of Professor Berriedale Keith, who argued that a Prime Minister could decline the invitation to form a government,

> and he ought so to decline if constitutional propriety under the British system does not mark out his appointment as right and proper on the part of the sovereign. When, therefore, he accepts office, he assumes therewith the duty of defending the formation of the new ministry,[1]

1. A.B. Keith, *The British Cabinet System* (2nd ed. by N.H. Gibbs, 1952), p.277.

including, it seems, the circumstances of the fall of his predecessor in so far as this involved the Monarch. Keith here quotes with approval the statement made by Peel when he became Prime Minister in 1834 after Melbourne's apparent dismissal by the King: 'I am, by my acceptance of office, responsible for the removal of the late Government.'[1] Clearly a Prime Minister is solely responsible (in both senses) for accepting the invitation to assume power, just as the Monarch alone is culpable for issuing the invitation in the first place, or for dismissing the previous Government. The doctrine that the Prime Minister and not the Monarch should be accountable for the latter is a pure fiction[2] which, today, is most unlikely to divert attention and criticism (if any there be) away from the Monarch. The doctrine did not have this protective effect in 1931 when the King was criticised, rightly or wrongly, for his part in the selection of Mr Ramsay MacDonald to head the National Government of that year, nor was it offered as a defence of George V by those most directly concerned.

To say that ministerial responsibility does not apply to the selection of a Prime Minister is not, however, to claim that the Monarch has complete discretion subject to no constitutional rules. It is generally agreed that other rules do operate, although their precise nature is debatable. A further distinction might be drawn here between substantive and procedural rules. Instances of the former are that a Monarch should not publicly appear to favour one political party or policy, or that the powers of the Crown should (very broadly speaking) be used only to further the aims of, or at least in such a way as to secure acceptance by, a parliamentary majority. The trouble about rules of this sort is that, crucial and fundamental though they may be, they provide canons of judgment, once the deed is done, rather than unambiguous guides to action by a Monarch seeking to behave constitutionally. How is the Monarch to decide what will appear partisan, or what will be acceptable to the majority? How can she avoid mistakes which will lead to criticism and, possibly, her unwilling involvement in political controversy? It is to answer this type of question that procedural rules may be required, though the distinction is of course only one of degree. The supreme but not the only example of such a rule is the principle of ministerial responsibility. Generally speaking the Monarch will be fulfilling the substantive rules mentioned, or (which is sufficient) will be accepted as so doing, if she acts in the way advised by her Ministers, i.e. follows a prescribed procedure in using her legal powers. It is the lack of precision about

1. op. cit., p. 273, and see p. 53 below.
2. Sir Ivor Jennings, *Cabinet Government* (3rd ed.), p. 449.

the procedural rules relevant to the selection of a Prime Minister which has given rise to uncertainty in this sphere.

Accepted procedural rules appear to be that the person selected must have the support of a majority in the House of Commons (if need be, after a new general election), and that the Monarch must 'secure the strongest Government in the minimum time'[1] while still observing the need for public impartiality. Most frequently, under the two-party system, all these requirements are met easily by sending for the Leader of the Opposition or of the majority party, as the case may be, upon the fall of a government—as happened, for example, in 1945 and 1951. Here the facts are such as to allow of no other choice. There was until recently one situation in which the Monarch might be called upon to exercise a degree of discretion but even this has now in practice been removed as the result of party political developments that took place between 1957 and 1965.

5. *The example of 1957*

This situation arose when a Prime Minister died in office or resigned for personal reasons, that is to say, when a vacancy occurred which was not accompanied by any change in the position of the parties. Even then, there might sometimes be no room for choice, as when Sir Anthony Eden succeeded Sir Winston Churchill. But when Sir Anthony retired in his turn in 1957, the Queen was not presented with any one obvious successor. Under such circumstances it was normally assumed that, although the Monarch would probably seek advice in order to discover what persons would be acceptable to the party in power, yet for the final choice she alone was morally and constitutionally responsible. It was clear, however, that an unwise or ill-advised Monarch might conceivably act in a manner which could be construed as partial, in that it appeared to reflect a royal preference for one particular group within the party. It is true, and important, that a party in a majority is able to reject any selection of which it does not approve—if it is prepared to undergo the internal conflict this would probably entail. A royal 'mistake' is not final; but it could still harm the Monarch's own reputation. To prevent this there must exist rules capable of serving as effective guides to action. In 1957, on Sir Anthony Eden's resignation, the Queen apparently sought and acted upon the advice of Sir Winston Churchill[2] and Lord Salisbury, both elder statesmen of the Conservative Party who had

1. ibid., pp. 20–58.

2. In a speech at Woodford in 1959 Sir Winston Churchill said, 'I recommended Mr Macmillan and was most delighted to see it was acted upon' (*The Times*, 7 January 1959).

themselves no personal ambitions at stake, and who appeared to have the confidence of their own party. At the same time the Labour Party took the opportunity of outlining the procedure it wished to be adopted in the selection of a Labour Prime Minister under comparable conditions. It declared that the Monarch should make no selection until a new Leader had been elected by the Parliamentary Labour Party in the same way as a Leader is chosen when the Party is in opposition. The Labour Party, thus, had given notice that it would not be prepared to accept a Leader chosen for it by the Monarch. The Conservatives, on the other hand, appeared still to accept traditional methods of selection. It is to be doubted, however, whether they would have done so had the Monarch exercised a wide personal discretion without seeking the advice of Conservative elders.' Both parties, nevertheless, seemed concerned to limit or even abolish the Monarch's culpability in this situation, and to insist upon a new procedural rule of what might be called 'party responsibility'. Such a 'rule' should not conflict with authority and precedent which require, essentially, only that the person selected be acceptable to the party in question. What it does is extend the requirements to include methods of selection which should virtually guarantee that the 'proper' choice is made for each party. To acknowledge this rule should thus have the double advantage of eliminating any appearance of royal partiality in selecting a Prime Minister on these occasions, and of ensuring that the parties obtain the leaders they want by the methods they want.

Reluctance to accept this conclusion may stem from a desire to have precisely the same rules applied to the rather different circumstances obtaining when there are three or more parties to be reckoned with. Under these conditions different procedural rules will probably

1. Mr Harold Macmillan has also described these events in an interview (*The Listener*, 13 May 1971). He said:

'Eden was too ill to do anything but just resign and he was neither asked his opinion nor volunteered it.

'*The Queen didn't ask him?*'

'No, she's not bound to. She saw Churchill and Salisbury. Salisbury reported that this was the view—with, I think, only one exception—of all the Cabinet: for me. They then asked, I think, some of the Party, the Party leaders and people in the Party organisation, who seemed to have the same view. And this was the advice that they gave. But that night I did nothing. There was nothing I could do. And so I just sat in my room and read *Pride and Prejudice*, very good book, and waited. I didn't want to see any of my colleagues because I didn't want to look as if I was canvassing, and I didn't go to the Treasury the next morning, as I thought it might be awkward, with people stopping you, and I heard nothing about it at all until at about 11 o'clock, on that next day or whatever the day was, I got a message from Sir Michael Adeane, the Queen's Private Secretary.'

be required to achieve the same substantial ends. It would clearly, for example, have been of little practical value to a President of the Fourth French Republic merely to have told him 'to send for the Leader of the Opposition' or even 'of the largest party not supporting the previous government'. And in fact a different set of (non-legal) guiding rules developed.[1]

A significant point is that if it is necessary to form a coalition government (as it normally was in the Fourth Republic) there may arise a situation in which the Monarch is or seems called upon to exercise a significant degree of personal discretion with little guidance as to the best way to perform her constitutional duties.

6. *The example of 1931*

Coalition governments in Britain are not as rare as is sometimes thought. Six times in this century governments have been formed, either on a multi-party basis or by a single minority party with the support of another (in 1915, 1916, 1924, 1929, 1931, and 1940), although the first of these should perhaps not be counted in that it was formed without any immediately preceding resignation. So far as can be judged from the published accounts, however, in all cases except that of 1931 the Monarch in fact had no significant discretion, the decision having been made for him by negotiation and agreement among the parties. It has even been argued that the one exception should not properly be so regarded.[2] The formation of the National Government of 1931 has, however, long been thought by both its defenders and critics to have been in some degree the result of the King's discretionary decision. The ensuing controversy raised a constitutional problem of some interest.

That King George V acted within the established rules is no longer seriously in dispute. On the other hand this has not saved him from criticism. Mr MacDonald's acceptance of office as Prime Minister of the new National Government was denounced by the overwhelming majority of his own party, which refused to support the new administration. Given the belief that the King had had some choice and influence in the matter, it is not surprising that doubts should have been cast upon the wisdom or impartiality of his decision. Mr Bassett has argued,[3] as have others, that such criticism is purely partisan, and that the King acted solely in the national interest. No grounds exist for thinking that the King had any other concern than to further the

1. P. Williams, 'Crisis in France: A Political Institution', VII *Cambridge Journal* 1 (1953), pp. 36–50.
2. R. Bassett, *1931: Political Crisis* (1958).
3. op. cit.

national interest, but opinions will often differ as to what the national interest demands. When such differences exist, then to embrace any one view of the national interest must necessarily seem less than fully impartial. When, moreover, that view is shared by some of the major political parties but not by all (as happened in 1931), then to accept it will necessarily be partisan, in the literal sense, whatever the intrinsic wisdom of the view. To defend as well as to attack action taken in furtherance of the view will also be partisan. The argument does not, therefore, necessarily avoid the need to question the adequacy of the existing rules as a defence of the Monarch's detached status.

If a constitutional problem exists here, and not everyone would agree that it does, it relates to the possibility of devising more effective methods whereby to keep the Monarch free from political controversy. To devise a mandatory procedure providing for the consultation of political parties would be difficult and probably not generally acceptable.[1] Another procedural 'rule' has, however, played a large part in the arguments about MacDonald's selection. The King's choice has been widely defended because it was agreed to and finally advised by the Leader or Acting-Leader of each of the three major political parties, even although MacDonald's initial reluctance had evidently to be overcome by persuasion on the part of his new colleagues and the King. But though this fact may be relevant to an assessment of the wisdom of the King's action, it would seem, by the canons of constitutional behaviour then generally recognised, to be irrelevant to the discussion of its constitutional propriety. It may be, however, that monarchs, in their efforts to remain above party politics and to avoid involvement in political controversy, have adopted the practice of seeking and acting upon the advice of the official party Leaders in the selection of coalition Prime Ministers, just as they have appeared to act upon the advice of party spokesmen in other circumstances.

7. *The example of 1963*

The selection of Mr Macmillan's successor presented more difficulties than did his own selection in 1957. Essentially this was because the Conservative Party was more deeply divided about a larger number of 'contestants' and because there was no suitable elder statesman available to give authoritative advice to the Monarch. All sections of the Party seemed to agree only that the real decision must be taken by and within the Party itself. Certainly all factions behaved as if the

1. cf. G. C. Moodie, 'The Monarch and the Selection of a Prime Minister: A Re-examination of the Crisis of 1931' (5 *Political Studies*, 1, 1957), and the criticisms advanced in Mr Bassett's *1931: Political Crisis*, at pp. 370–5.

Party's preference was conclusive, and Sir Alec Douglas-Home seems in fact to have been chosen by the Party, albeit under the skilful guidance of his predecessor. But the uncertainties about the appropriate inner-party machinery still left room for doubt about the actual and desirable role of the Monarch. It may be, therefore, that the events of October 1963 accelerated the acceptance of 'party responsibility' as the proper procedural rule. Incidentally, the example of 1963 may have been important also because it revived an older procedure for dealing with situations where it is difficult to identify the next Premier. On this occasion the effect of the Monarch's Act was to emphasise party responsibility by, initially, only inviting someone to form an administration and not appointing him until his success is assured. But this has now become unnecessary.

8. *The example of 1965*

After the Conservative Party was sent into opposition by the general election of 1964 it examined its own procedure for selecting a Leader and, early in 1965, adopted an elaborate system of election.[1] The procedure was soon tested when Sir Alec Douglas-Home resigned. Mr Edward Heath was thereupon elected to succeed him after a decorous contest. It seems that the Conservative Party, like the Labour Party, will insist upon electing its own Leader by the same method even should the need arise when it is in office. There is thus, apparently, no possibility that the Monarch will exercise a genuine choice in the appointment of future Prime Ministers of one-party governments nor, by implication, of coalition governments. In both cases 'party responsibility' seems likely to provide the operative procedural rule—at least for as long as the present two major parties continue to dominate British politics.

1. The system provides for a ballot of the Party in the House of Commons conducted, if necessary, in three stages. A candidate is elected on a first ballot if he receives an overall majority plus 15 per cent more of the votes cast than any other candidate. If no candidate satisfies these conditions, new nominations are received and a second ballot held, at which a candidate is elected if he receives an overall majority. If at that stage no candidate secures a majority a third ballot, of the top three candiates, is held at which voters express a first and second preference. The candidate with the lowest number of first preferences is then eliminated and the votes of those giving him as their first preference are redistributed among the two remaining candidates in accordance with their second preference. Only the first stage of this procedure was necessary in 1965 as Mr Reginald Maudling (who received 133 votes as against Mr Heath's 150 and Mr Enoch Powell's 15) stood down after the first ballot.

The candidate elected by this procedure is thereafter presented to, and presumably in theory elected by, the party meeting. It was stated in 1965 that if the party meeting were to reject the Commons choice the election procedure would be initiated again with fresh nominations.

4

MINISTERS AND PARLIAMENT

1. *The meaning of ministerial responsibility*

With the exception of those few acts of political significance which remain the personal prerogatives of the Crown, Ministers are responsible for all acts of government. We have seen in speaking of Ministers and the Crown that such a statement may be interpreted in several ways. Comparable difficulties arise in speaking of the relations between Ministers and the legislature. In ordinary discourse the word 'responsible' has a range of nuances. We say 'He is a responsible person.' 'Who is responsible for this?' 'They are overburdened with responsibility.' A man who is not 'responsible' for his actions in one sense may yet be 'responsible' for an accident in another. At times the word is used merely to attribute an action to its author; or it may be used to indicate a relationship or division of function between persons who are members of an organised group; or it may be used with a moral flavour to allot praise or blame. Where it describes a relationship between persons, the relation is not necessarily one of subordination or answerability to a superior. Two people may have joint 'responsibilities' in which neither is subordinate to the other. In the United States, for example, the responsibilities of President and Congress are co-ordinate in this way and neither is answerable to the other. But in principle 'responsibility' depends covertly or overtly on the notion of a rule alleged to govern the duties of those involved. The rule may be a legal one, a political one, a social one, or perhaps a rule of the speaker's own making.

In both ordinary talk and in political discussion, it is not always easy, as we have seen, to distinguish the appropriate nuance. In the constitutional sphere 'ministerial responsibility' is certainly used to convey a number of different implications. In one sense it states the absence of legal irresponsibility. Since the Monarch is not legally answerable in person for the acts of the Crown, legal responsibility must be assumed by his servants and Ministers. Here the duty or responsibility flows from a legal rule. In another sense ministerial responsibility exists because of the conventional and non-legal rule, that the Government is subordinate to Parliament. (Historically this subordination was also legal in its character since it might be enforced by the instrument of impeachment of Ministers at the instance of the Commons. The liability of individual Ministers to impeachment seems, in fact, in the eighteenth century to have been the primary sense attached to ministerial responsibility.) In a third sense Ministers are responsible morally for culpable actions in the same way as everybody else. The statement that Ministers are responsible for their actions in the sense of being constitutionally accountable to Parliament and liable to suffer the penalties, if any, of parliamentary disapproval does not in itself convey any judgment as to the culpability of their actions. Nor is it always clear from the context of a discussion whether any personal moral responsibility is implied or not. In 1835 Sir Robert Peel stated that by his acceptance of office of Prime Minister the responsibility for the change of government was transferred from the Crown to himself. Since he added, out of respect for his own character, that he had taken no part in instigating the dismissal of Lord Melbourne's Government he was clearly far from accepting any personal responsibility, except perhaps in the somewhat diluted sense that he had not dissociated himself from the transaction to the extent of refusing office. Sometimes this sense is even more diluted, as for example when a Minister accepts 'responsibility' for the act of a ministerial predecessor with which he is in personal disagreement. In 1957, for example, the action of the Home Office in disclosing certain information obtained by the police in the course of tapping telephone conversations was raised in the House.[1] The disclosure had been authorised by the Home Secretary's predecessor, Viscount Tenby. Mr Butler, the Home Secretary, was not prepared to defend the action on its merits, but stated that he accepted responsibility for it. Here the term 'responsibility' is almost entirely empty. It is true that Mr Butler had the usual obligation to explain and answer questions; but one can explain and give information about actions which one repudiates. Here, evidently, the only cash-value in the statement that the Minister accepted responsibility was that he was the appropriate recipient of parliamentary questions and the person from whom to demand undertakings for the future. But that is hardly responsibility for the actions themselves, and there

1. cf. Cmnd. 283 (1957), *Report of the Committee of Privy Councillors appointed to inquire into the interception of communications.*

seems no reason in principle why a Minister should accept responsibility for courses of action initiated by predecessors which he wishes to discontinue.

2. *Collective responsibility*

The concept of the King's servants and Ministers as a collective entity is of course connected with the growth of Cabinet Government and solidarity in the late eighteenth and nineteenth centuries, though estimates differ as to the point in time at which the implications of the modern doctrine were recognised as obligatory. The habit of calling the Ministers who carried on the King's Government 'The Government' appears to have been an even later linguistic development. Edward Freeman wrote in 1872:

> I may mark a change of language which has happened within my own memory. . . . We now familiarly speak . . . of the body of Ministers actually in power, the body known to the Constitution but wholly unknown to the law, by the name of 'the Government'. We speak of 'Mr Gladstone's Government' or 'Mr Disraeli's Government'. I can myself remember the time when such a form of words was unknown, when 'Government' still meant 'Government' by King, Lords and Commons.[1]

Modern discussions of the collective responsibility of the Government do not always distinguish clearly between, on the one hand, stating a rule about the constitutional homogeneity of the administration and, on the other, allotting responsibility in a moral sense to individuals. The distinction is important for example in describing the 'responsibility' of Cabinet Members in wartime who are excluded from an inner War Cabinet or Council or of Ministers in normal times who do not sit in the Cabinet. Before the growth of homogeneous Cabinet responsibility in its modern sense, the distinction between what was sometimes called the 'nominal' and the 'efficient' or 'confidential' Cabinet marked out a clear distinction between the moral responsibilities of inner and outer Ministers. Moreover, whilst responsibility suggested impeachment, even inner Cabinet Members could not easily be thought of as liable merely in respect of the actions of their colleagues.[2] Something of these uncertainties infects the modern doctrine. 'Once a policy is adopted by the Cabinet,' one author writes, 'all Ministers share the responsibility for it. But their actual degree of responsibility varies as between the Cabinet Members . . . forming and carrying out the decisions and ordinary Cabinet

1. *The growth of the English Constitution from the Earliest Times* (3rd ed. 1876), pp. 123–4.

2. cf. Anson, *Law and Custom of the Constitution* (4th ed., vol. 2, pt. 1), pp. 114–18.

Members who take no active part in doing so.'[1] It is not clear from this formulation whether the constitutional rule stated in the first sentence is modified or not by the differences between Cabinet Members pointed out in the succeeding sentence. In 1940 Mr Winston Churchill was acceptable to both parties since, in Sir Ivor Jennings's words, he 'had not been considered responsible for the disaster in Norway (though as First Lord of the Admiralty he had accepted his share of collective responsibility)'.[2] But what does 'acceptance' of this kind amount to? How much impact does differing culpability in fact have upon the constitutional rule? In the words of another leading authority, Ministers who do not sit in the Cabinet are 'bound by Cabinet decisions and must refrain from criticising or opposing them in public. But on matters outside their departmental responsibilities they are not consulted in advance. It may be said that such Ministers share the consequences of collective responsibility but that their actual responsibility is not the same. Their role is negative and that of the Cabinet positive.'[3] If responsibility is taken in the formal constitutional sense, there would seem, granted collective governmental responsibility, to be no clear distinction to be drawn between Ministers inside and those outside the Cabinet. To *be* responsible in this sense simply is to share the consequences of responsibility—namely to be subject to the rule that no member of the Government may properly remain a member and dissociate himself from its policies (except on occasions when the Government permits a free vote in the House). If, on the other hand, the moral culpability or praiseworthiness of individuals is in question, there is no point in placing the boundary-line precisely between Cabinet and non-Cabinet Members. There is no reason to suppose that all Members of the Cabinet itself are actually or 'positively' responsible in a moral sense for any particular governmental action. A majority of the Cabinet may simply have acquiesced in an action instigated by two or three, or outside influence may have been decisive. If by 'actual' responsibility is meant the moral marks allotted by the speaker or by posterity, then there is no reason for treating the distinction between Cabinet and non-Cabinet Members as having any special relevance at all.

The substance of the Government's collective responsibility could be defined as its duty to submit its policy to and defend its policy before the House of Commons, and to resign if defeated on an issue of confidence. The defeat of any substantial bill is nowadays regarded as a loss of confidence. This was not always so. It was argued (for

1. W. Yu, *The English Cabinet System* (1939), p. 375.
2. *Cabinet Government* (3rd ed.), p. 27.
3. E. C. S. Wade and G. Phillips, *Constitutional Law* (7th ed.), p. 90.

example by Lord Macaulay) that the ability to provide a stable administration—being the primary function of government—did not entail a duty to avoid defeat on mere legislative proposals. There may be something to be said for this view, though it is a principle which politicians in a predominantly two-party House of Commons might now find difficult to sustain in the face of the notion of Parliament as a legislative machine directed by Ministers and powered by a legislative mandate. The modern practice, however, is a stricter one than that of carrying major legislative measures. For governments now regard it as politically incumbent upon them to avoid defeat in the Commons on any issue whatsoever, whether on the floor of the House or in Committee. (Resignation does not, of course, follow upon a chance defeat in Committee, but the matter is regarded as one whose consequences must be put right at the earliest opportunity.) It is not perhaps self-evident that such a rigidity of principle is necessary to the successful working of the parliamentary system, or that it is required by an constitutional convention. In the Commons' debate of January 1958 on the procedure of the House some back-bench arguments in favour of a conscious relaxation of the practice were heard. It was suggested, for example, that the Government might 'let it be known that on all minor matters of the Committee stage of Bills, wherever they are taken, it will not be regarded as a world-shaking event justifying the resignation of the Government . . . if the Government are defeated'. The benefits, it was said, might include more freedom of action for individual Members of Parliament, and some lightening of the physical responsibility of attendance to vote in divisions. The Home Secretary, replying to the debate, thought that it was necessary for Members to face a certain amount of discomfort in playing to the rules of the parliamentary contest. 'We are here,' he said, 'in a struggle for power. If we started to reach some sort of agreement between the parties that there could be a defeat of the Government of the day, it is doubtful if the parliamentary system would work.'[1] There is perhaps a suspicion of circularity in the argument here. That a defeat for the Government is a defeat in the parliamentary struggle for power is so because all such defeats are regarded as counting adversely according to the existing conventional practice. It is not inherent in the nature of an already artificial struggle that its rules could not be otherwise than they are. The contest for power is not, as matters stand, conducted without restriction. When, for example in the Parliament of 1950–1, discomforting consequences were seen to follow from attempts to bring about snap defeats of the Government by late-night prayers against statutory

1. 581 HC Deb., c. 760.

instruments, it was not thought improper to suggest procedural remedies for the inconveniences to Members and thus in a minor way deliberately to relax the rules of the parliamentary struggle for power. It is hard to see why a voluntary loosening of conventional practices on a minor scale by a government with a safe majority, or an extension of the number of occasions on which a free vote is permitted, must be incompatible with the principles of the parliamentary system. Any extension of free voting is admittedly often opposed either on the ground that it exposes Members to outside pressures—a view which suggests its own remedy—or on the ground that 'governments should govern' and not evade their responsibility. It is slightly curious that 'responsibility' which originally stood for the amenability of the Crown and its servants to legislative control should have come to stand in this sense for an assertion of the executive's independence of parliamentary control.

Free votes suggest some further questions about the nature of the Government's collective responsibility to Parliament. Is the nature of responsibility to the Commons affected by the fact that the House is voting, when the Whips are off, as a collection of individuals rather than as the organised forum of party views? Moreover, what is the nature of the Government's responsibility when a decision reached in the Commons in this way is opposed to the majority view of the upper House? Both these questions emerged in 1956 when the House of Lords rejected the proposed abolition of the death penalty after it had been carried on a free vote in the Commons. It was strongly urged by Members supporting abolition that the Government's constitutional duty was to prefer the opinion of the lower House and to afford facilities for that view to prevail by carrying it against the Lords' opposition, under the procedure provided by the Parliament Acts. This view was not accepted by the Government or by those who opposed abolition. An intractable deadlock between the two Houses had not, it was argued, been reached, and the conditions under which the Parliament Acts had previously been invoked—namely a deadlock between an elected Government and the Commons on the one hand, and the Lords on the other—did not in this case exist. The Government was not as a government committed to, or in favour of, the course indicated by the Commons' vote. Some general arguments in support of this view were advanced in the editorial columns of *The Times*. The use of the Parliament Acts was not required, *The Times* argued, by any constitutional convention, and any such use would be adapting those Acts for a purpose quite foreign to the intention with which they were passed. The legislative authority in Great Britain was not vested in a single chamber, or even two. It belonged to Queen, Lords, and Commons and the Constitution required every effort to be made to bring all three into harmony before emergency measures to give preference to one were applied. The Government, it was added, were the umpires and should make up their own minds.[1]

Here is a problem generated by the informal and debatable nature of British constitutional conventions. From these general principles arguments could be marshalled on both sides. In the event, since they were backed by the Government, the views of those who supported the thesis advanced by *The Times* prevailed. The argument, none the less, deserves some scrutiny in isolation from the details of the capital punishment controversy. The view is often advanced, for example, that a government has the right to take an independent umpire's stance and to lead and influence opinion as against the electorate (though perhaps this is more than an umpire might be expected to do). This in turn may be defended on the ground that the Government consists of Members of Parliament who are not delegates but elected to govern in ways in which as men of known party principles may seem best to them. It may be obviously true that when a government carries with it the support of a majority of the Commons, as in all normal cases, its authority must prevail as against any contrary view. But these are different propositions from that which asserts that the government without a majority in the Commons preserves the right and duty of independent judgment, on a matter committed to a free vote of the House, as against a majority of the Commons as a whole. In what sense does such a view manifest the principle of ministerial responsibility to Parliament?

The Times ventured, in addition, on an argument which seems even more disputable. The Government's responsibility for finding a way out of the disagreement could be based, it was suggested, upon the fact that the Commons had voted according to their individual consciences and not as representatives of their constituents. It followed, *The Times* argued, that 'Lords and Members of Parliament are on an equal footing as so many individuals'. This seems a surprising doctrine. In the first place, the co-ordinate status of the three elements of the legislature is legally undeniable, but since the conventions of the constitution are, as Dicey declared, directed towards securing a supremacy of the will of the elected element, it is far from clear that the Lords are entitled as a matter of constitutional principle to be counted as politically co-ordinate legislative elements along with the Commons and Crown (whose entitlement is more remote still). But more important: in what sense can a vote of the Commons be

1. *The Times*, 24 October 1956; cf. 631 HC Deb., c. 1443 (1960).

regarded as possessing less authority by reason of being a free vote? It is not necessary to invoke the Burkeian view that the exercise of individual conscience adds rather than detracts from the moral authority of the Commons' vote. But *vis-à-vis* the Lords at least its authority can hardly be *less* than that of a vote by members holding their individual consciences in abeyance.

If these objections have any force they provide a reason for suggesting that a government which holds itself totally absolved from following a course indicated by a free vote in the House is evading a constitutional responsibility to the Commons. Could it be urged in reply that responsibility was preserved in the present instance since the majority which found itself at odds with Ministers could have brought the Government down by opposing their subsequent measures and in fact refrained from doing so? This is certainly true, but it is true in practically every conceivable situation. If it were admitted in exculpation it would seem to follow that a government whilst it remained the government never could be convicted of evading responsibility on a particular issue, and that no meaning could be attached to the suggestion. For Members do not express disapproval by defeating their leaders except on the most fundamental issue (and possibly not even then). Perhaps, therefore, we should say that the only responsibility of Ministers is to hold their party together. But this, whatever its soundness as a maxim of political strategy, sounds decidedly odd as a constitutional convention.

The development of party solidarity thus poses a delicate question about the convention of responsibility. The convention states, in its original form, the conditions upon which a government may hold and forfeit office. Yet everyone knows that when governments nowadays go out of office, it is not the operation of the convention which bring this about, but the decision of the party in power to submit itself to a general election—an apt illustration of the way in which changes in the number and nature of the political parties may transform the operation of a conventional rule. The sanction envisaged in the principle of accountability—namely the House of Commons as an entity withdrawing its confidence from Ministers accordingly as it approves or disapproves of their proposals—is for all practical purposes simply not in operation. Its existence is a kind of limbo-existence. Yet some reflection is cast into the world of political reality, since the Government customarily behaves in a way which would be quite mystifying to an observer who knew only that the majority party was in possession of the right to use the legislative machinery of the Commons. Both Ministers and back-benchers make frequent references to 'the House' as an entity; the Government sometimes genuinely defers to 'the feeling of the House' (admittedly with an appreciation of potential dissident feeling on the ministerial benches); and there always remains the possibility that there may be further changes in the party situation or that some catastrophic issue may throw party divisions into confusion and revive the traditional sanction. But are these good enough reasons for using the traditional language of governmental accountability in the present situation? An answer may perhaps be postponed since precisely this question has recently been asked about the convention of individual ministerial responsibility.

3. *Individual responsibility*

A similar problem may be stated in the light of the solid party majority about the individual responsibility of Ministers to that about the Government's collective responsibility. Ministers, it is said, are responsible to Parliament as individuals for the work of their departments and the sanction for mismanagement is the House's demand for the resignation of the Minister. Yet when resignations do occur, the determining factor is in practice the alienation by a Minister of his party colleagues rather than the operation of the constitutional principle. What then are we to say of the rule which is often stated in the form that there exists a liability on a Minister to resign for errors in administration not connected with the general policy of his Cabinet colleagues? The efficacy of this principle as a sanction upon Ministers was strongly denied by Sidney Low half a century ago. The House cannot in fact, he pointed out, get rid of one Minister of whose conduct it disapproves, without getting rid of the Government, if its intended victim is sheltered behind the shield of joint responsibility. Acts unconnected with government policy can be treated by the administration as raising a question of confidence, and moreover a Minister, besides being aware of this, is also aware that when he does lose his office, his fall is likely to be the result of other ministerial shortcomings bearing no necessary relation to his own departmental conduct. 'He may,' Low wrote,

> have cost the country thousands of lives and millions of pounds, launching an ill-arranged expedition into the heart of a distant continent, too late for it to be of any use; and his defeat may eventually be brought about because his colleagues have decided—perhaps in opposition to his own wishes—to put an unpopular tax on bread or on beer.[1]

With some small substitution of examples, Ministers experience similar immunities and contingencies today.

1. *The Governance of England* (1904), pp. 148–9.

Professor S. E. Finer has underlined the point with great thoroughness in an examination of the ministerial resignations which have taken place in the last century.[1] Factors which negative the punitive effect of the convention he categorises as: first, the reappointment of a Minister who has resigned to another post; secondly, 'timely removal' of a Minister by a Cabinet or ministerial reshuffle before the issue of resignation becomes a pressing one; and thirdly, collective solidarity exerted to protect a Minister unpopular with the Opposition. Where a government refrains from the last of these devices the explanation may be either (as has been suggested in the case of Sir Samuel Hoare's resignation in 1935) that it may wish to use the convention of individual responsibility to divest itself of collective responsibility for an unpopular policy, or that maladministration may be complicated by an issue which cuts across normal party ideologies. The resignation of Sir Thomas Dugdale in 1954 following the debate on the Crichel Down inquiry could be presented as an example of the second kind. The exercise of collectivist powers over land was not one calculated to call upon the normal loyalties of the Conservative Government's supporters. The only generalisation which can be made, Professor Finer argues, is that 'If the Minister is yielding, his Prime Minister unbending, and his party out for blood —no matter how serious or trivial the reason—the Minister will find himself without Parliamentary support.' Is there then, he asks, apart from this mere truism, any convention of resignation at all? A prescriptive rule must be based on an observed uniformity of events plus an expectation that it will continue. There is no such uniformity of events. Therefore there can be no rule based on it. The convention of individual responsibility means, Professor Finer suggests, not that a Minister is answerable *for* his conduct, in the sense that he may be held censurable and constrained to resign, but only that he is answerable *to* the House, in the sense of having a duty to explain and answer questions about the activities of his department before it.

This is indeed a convincing rebuttal of the belief that a pattern of resignations can be found in recent times which fits the idealised mould of a punitive sanction exercised against an erring Minister by the Commons. It may be observed that it would be equally impossible, on the basis of an observed sequence of effective sanctions, to say that the Government as a whole is censurable or responsible to the Commons. The case would be equally strong, if the implications of this thesis were accepted, for saying either that the convention

1. 'The Individual Responsibility of Ministers', *Public Administration*, Winter 1956, p. 377.

about collective responsibility, in so far as it involves the likelihood of censure, is consistently frustrated, or else that it does not exist at all. But how conclusive is the argument from the relative absence of typical instances of the convention in operation? Logically speaking, of course, the infrequency in its operation might be an indication of the sanction's supreme efficacy in inducing caution and good behaviour in Ministers. The usefulness of describing the convention as existing may depend in part on an estimate of the permanence of the present party situation.

It may of course be maintained both of governments and of Ministers individually that their 'responsibility', 'accountability', or 'answerability' imply merely the obligation of Ministers, collectively and individually, to meet Parliament and provide information about their policies. If this is what 'answerable' means in the constitutional sphere, it must be allowed that the usage is slightly eccentric. 'Explaining' and 'answering to' are, in ordinary speech, terms with an entirely different flavour. The distinction between 'answerable *to*' and 'answerable *for*' is difficult to maintain. Where there is no relation of authority one may 'answer', but it is hardly appropriate to speak of being *answerable* at all—either 'to' or 'for'. We may, for example, answer questions about our health or explain that we are in good health, but we do not normally 'answer to' anybody for our health. A Minister at the dispatch box, answering to the House, is at least acting as if his explanations were to a body with authority. He is not just reciting a part, or treating Members as curious or interested bystanders, or performing as a kind of parliamentary press and information office. It is certainly true that censure by the House is not (as Professor Finer persuasively indicates) an effective remedy for administrative mismanagement. Nevertheless, that Ministers are constitutionally liable (as distinct from politically likely) to receive parliamentary censure may be a part of the theory of the constitution whose denial we ought not—in Mr Morrison's phrase—to be 'shouting to the world'. There is indeed much parliamentary behaviour and language which is comprehensible only on the assumption of punitive authority on the part of the House, as distinct from a mere right to information. Governments which shield unpopular Ministers do not at any rate ever do so on the explicit ground that no such convention as answerability for departmental action is known to them, and on many occasions the convention in its punitive form seems to be taken for granted by Members of Parliament on both sides of the House. Perhaps one of the clearest occasions in recent years was in fact the resignation of Sir Thomas Dugdale, Minister of Agriculture in 1954, after the criticism of his Department's handling of land at Crichel

Down. At least one Member was certain that 'the House of Commons is the arbiter in determining whether a Minister should be required to resign or not'.[1] The Home Secretary, speaking in the debate after the Minister's resignation, referred to the Minister's duty to 'render an account of his stewardship', and Sir Thomas himself said: 'I have told the House of the action which has been taken and which will be taken . . . to make a recurrence of the present case impossible. . . . Having now had this opportunity of rendering account to Parliament of the actions which I thought fit to take, I have, as the Minister responsible during this period, tendered my resignation to the Prime Minister.'[2]

The implications for the doctrine of individual responsibility may be different accordingly as a Minister's resignation follows conduct which he is prepared to defend or conduct which he admits to be erroneous. The resignation of Mr Hugh Dalton in 1947 followed an improper though trivial and inadvertent disclosure of a budget proposal. That of Mr J. H. Thomas in 1936 followed allegations of a similar kind which, though disputed by Mr Thomas, were upheld by a tribunal of inquiry. Sir Thomas Dugdale's resignation speech contained a strong defence of his policy, but conceded administrative failings. Each of these, therefore, may be attributed to the doctrine of individual responsibility. Sir Samuel Hoare in 1935, on the other hand, was not prepared to concede that his actions had been erroneous. Nor, according to his own account, did the initiative for the Minister's resignation come from the Cabinet, except in the sense that it was forced upon him by the change of Cabinet policy on the proposals he had submitted to it. Baldwin found him, Hoare relates, 'determined to defend the plan, and in consequence to resign'. 'Baldwin himself,' he adds, 'never suggested resignation to me. In fact he would much have preferred that I should have fallen in with the Cabinet's wish for a recantation and have remained in the Government. My decision was, however, final.'[3] In cases of this type the Minister's resignation might be described as due not to the doctrine of individual responsibility but to the convention of collective responsibility which prescribes resignation for members of the Government who find themselves unable to support its proposals.

It is noteworthy that on two of these occasions resignation followed a public inquiry, under an independent judicial chairman, into the activities of a Governmental department and that the Home Secre-

1. 530 HC Deb., 5s., c. 1268.
2. ibid., c. 1198.
3. Viscount Templewood, *Nine Troubled Years* (1954), p. 185.

tary stated as a general proposition in Sir Thomas Dugdale's case that the Government ought to regard itself as bound by the findings of fact reached at such inquiries.[1] One distinctive type of sanction upon Ministers, which is not often remarked upon, is to be seen therefore in the possibility—admittedly not a large one—that a government, on occasion at least, may yield to parliamentary or public pressure and set up either a parliamentary committee of inquiry or an investigation under the provisions of the Tribunals of Inquiry (Evidence) Act of 1921, and that the conduct of Ministers and Civil Servants may become the subject of a form of quasi-judicial inquiry. Inquisition of this nature is so rare a feature of the administrative process in this country as to appear almost un-English, and it cannot be supposed to be an ever-present element in Civil Service calculations. But such independent inquiries involving ministerial departmental conduct have taken place—for example in 1957 (under Lord Justice Parker), in 1948 (under Mr Justice Lynskey), and in 1963 (under Lords Radcliffe and Denning). Such proceedings are perhaps the nearest modern analogy to the form of responsibility once embodied in the risk of impeachment.

4. *Responsibility for Civil Servants*

There seems to be some uncertainty about the doctrine that Ministers are responsible for every act of their Civil Service subordinates. Sir Ivor Jennings in his *Cabinet Government* speaks of 'the responsibility of the Minister for every act done in his department'. In Mr Herbert Morrison's words, 'There can be no question whatever that Ministers are responsible for everything that their officers do.' The Minister 'is responsible for every stamp stuck on an envelope'.[2] Now it is clear in the light of earlier discussion of the term 'responsible' that such a statement might mean a number of things. It might mean that each act is legally to be considered that of the Minister. It might mean that the Minister must hold himself morally responsible for every act of his subordinates. Or it might mean that the Minister (and the Minister alone) is the constitutional mouthpiece through which departmental actions are to be defended or repudiated and from whom information is to be sought. In the last of these statements, at least, there is nothing which necessarily implies either that the Minister ought to be censured by Parliament if things outside his personal moral responsibility go wrong, or that a Minister need feel any obligation to accept parliamentary censure for such actions, or that a Minister may not repudiate (in the sense of disclaiming personal moral respon-

1. 530 HC Deb., 5s., c. 1296.
2. 530 HC Deb., 5s., c. 1278.

sibility) the wrongful actions of subordinates. The only senses in which he *cannot* repudiate such actions are the legal sense and the sense that the House if it wishes, and if it is permitted to, may express its displeasure. Nevertheless, the impression apt to be gathered from much popular discussion is that the political heads of departments suffer a liability to be at any time sacrificed on the altar of a rigid doctrine of vicarious ministerial responsibility—a doctrine which, whilst bearing harshly upon Ministers virtuous in their persons, remains necessary and healthful to preserve the Constitution from bureaucratic irresponsibility. But what would this imply? If it did not mean simply that censure or criticism by Parliament is possible whether it is deserved or not, it must imply that Ministers have a constitutional duty either to resign or to defend every action of their department as if it were done on the Minister's personal initiative. It seems clear that at the present time no such duty exists. In the Crichel Down debate, during which Sir Thomas Dugdale announced his resignation, the then Home Secretary, Sir David Maxwell Fyfe, conceded that when officials made mistakes or caused delays which did not involve an important issue of policy a Minister not personally involved might properly state that he would take corrective action in the department—thus clearly indicating his officials and not himself as the agents of the mischief. Moreover where action is taken of which the Minister disapproves and has no prior knowledge 'there is,' said the Home Secretary, 'no obligation on the part of the Minister to endorse what he believes to be wrong, or to defend what are clearly shown to be errors of his officers'.[1] Oddly enough, Sir David added that, having acknowledged the mistake, the Minister 'accepts the responsibility'. Clearly, beyond acting as the mouthpiece for information and apology, this is precisely what he does not do. Mr Herbert Morrison's views, both in the debate and in his book, *Government and Parliament*, are comparable. He, too, insists that though the consequences 'may be rather hard on a Minister from time to time', he 'must accept responsibility as if the act were his own'. Yet he has 'a perfect right to reveal the facts and to assure the House that he has taken suitable action'[2] where his specific orders have been disobeyed. On one such occasion a disobedient officer in the Home Office had been castigated in the House. 'I did not like doing it,' Mr Morrison added. 'The poor man sat in the Gallery over there. I think that that was legitimate—good

1. ibid., c. 1290; cf. the statement of Sir Anthony Eden on disciplinary action in the episode involving Commander Crabb (below, pp. 141–2).

2. *Government and Parliament. A Survey from the Inside* (1954), pp. 320–4.

for him, and, what is more important, good for everybody else.'[1] On another occasion referred to by Mr Morrison error was more widely shared. The wartime regulations made under the Act providing for the National Fire Service were never brought before Parliament. In the Minister's words, 'The Department forgot, I forgot, and . . . neither House of Parliament noticed.' A 'serious sin against the rights of parliamentary democracy had been committed'. Accordingly, Mr Morrison relates, he explained what had happened to the House, 'sincerely apologising "in italics" '[2] (why in italics, though?); and an Act of Indemnity was passed. Was this a mistake on a matter of policy? It might have been described as a merely technical legal point of no particular moment; or it might equally well have been described, as it was by the Minister himself (though perhaps with his tongue at least half-way into his cheek), as a thing of considerable constitutional import affecting the rights of citizens. And even if it were a matter of policy coming within the sphere of the Minister's knowledge, might not a Minister shift the responsibility from his shoulders, at least in the case where the rules he has laid down in his department have been disregarded or disobeyed? This involves a type of failure which Mr Morrison does not directly mention, but which was hinted at by Sir David Maxwell Fyfe—namely an omission to arrange the department's work in such a way that 'policy' matters are personally caught at some stage. The Minister 'can lay down rules by which it is ensured that matters of importance, of difficulty, or of political danger are brought to his attention'.[3] It is not always obvious whether an alleged ministerial failing can fairly be said to fall within this category or not. Matters involving political danger cannot easily be defined beforehand, and the most routine piece of clumsiness in exercising administrative discretion is capable if taken hold of by Members of Parliament of inflating itself overnight. However, the following conclusions seem fair. If culpable action within a department clearly falls into the sphere where reasonable diligence on the Minister's part in controlling his department would have led to his being personally aware of the issue then a failure to act can be construed as a *personal*[4] fault. If, on the other hand, it does not fall

1. 530 HC Deb., 5s., c. 1280.
2. *Government and Parliament*, p. 232.
3. 530 HC Deb., 5s., c. 1287.
4. That individual responsibility for alleged personal fault exists is illustrated by resignations such as those of Galbraith (1962) and Profumo (1963). Other recent examples fall into the category of 'collective responsibility resignations', e.g. those of Nutting and Boyle (1956), Lord Salisbury (1957), Thorneycroft (1958) and of Mayhew, Cousins, Herbison, Gunter, Lord Longford and Brown from the Wilson government of 1966–70.

within such a class of matters, or if deliberate disobedience has occurred, then the Minister may properly disclaim fault on behalf of himself. There seems no middle ground at all in which he must of necessity accept a vicarious guilt for the sins of his subordinates. The convention here, therefore, is more liberal than is often supposed, though the precise degrees of its liberality seem only to have become a matter for comment in fairly recent years.

5

THE COURTS AND THE LEGISLATIVE PROCESS

1. *Responsibility to Parliament*

Judges in cases involving departmental powers often remark that Ministers are responsible to Parliament for the conduct of their department and that any action taken in the department, whether by way of making legislative orders or by way of considering appeals against particular decisions, can be reviewed by Parliament. What moral about the controlling function of the courts follows from this statement? It seems clear that despite the judicial emphasis which has been given to parliamentary responsibility the answer to this question must be extremely uncertain. If any practical conclusion were seriously to be drawn it would hardly be possible to avoid assessing the weight to be given to the well-known facts of parliamentary life—to the Minister's protective armour in the Party Whip, for example, and the shortage of parliamentary time—matters which are not assessed or normally mentioned when 'Parliament' is referred to in the Law Reports. Even if continuous impartial legislative inquiry into the actions of each department were within the realm of possibility, it would not follow directly from this fact alone that no alternative or additional judicial control could have been envisaged by Parliament in delegating powers to Ministers and their departments. If Acts of Parliament were completely silent on the issue it would be as sensible to draw one conclusion as the other. In fact Acts of Parliament are not entirely silent; but they are not entirely explicit either, and various conclusions have been drawn by the Bench (often conflicting) about what Parliament 'must have intended'. Possibly the most notorious example is the disagreement between the majority of the House of Lords in *Liversidge v. Anderson*[1] and the dissenting judge, Lord Atkin, as to the nature of the powers conferred on the Home Secretary, Sir John Anderson, under the wartime Defence

1. [1942] AC 206. See also below at p. 130.

Regulations of 1939. Regulation 18B empowered the Home Secretary to intern persons whom he had 'reasonable cause' to believe to be of hostile origin or associations, and the issue raised by *Liversidge's* action alleging false imprisonment against the Home Secretary was whether the reasonableness of the Minister's action could be tested in the courts, or whether the Minister had merely to assert his subjective belief in the reasonableness of his action and defend himself before Parliament. Dismissing the appeal, the majority of the Law Lords argued that the matter was clearly one for executive discretion. 'I cannot myself believe,' said Viscount Maugham, 'that those responsible for the Order in Council could have contemplated for a moment the possibility of the action of the Secretary of State being subject to the discussion, criticism, and control of a judge in a court of law.' The Minister might be acting on confidential information and it could be inferred from his duty to report to Parliament that he was not to be considered as in the position of a minor administrative official such as a police constable. Lord Atkin, on the other hand, took the view that when either policemen or Ministers were required to have reasonable cause for action, the question was an objective one capable of being tested as an issue of fact in the courts. 'If a Minister has reasonable cause' could not, he argued, mean 'If a Minister thinks he has reasonable cause'. The discussion which followed *Liversidge's* case revealed fairly widespread differences of opinion about the inferences to be drawn from the regulations to which Parliament had given its approval. It was argued that both the Home Secretary and the Attorney-General had said in the House that they had not contemplated that decisions under the regulation should be open to review in the courts. On the other hand it could be said that that fact was not conclusive as to what had been in the mind of the Commons. Both Sir William Holdsworth and the editor of the *Law Quarterly Review*, Dr A. L. Goodhart, felt the decision of the majority to be both 'good law' and 'good common sense'. In a note written in 1942 Holdsworth argued that the Home Secretary's conduct was 'not a triable issue within the legal competence of a court'. It was 'not a justiciable, but a political or administrative issue'.[1]

The arguments here contain many of the features of later disputes about the interpretation of ministerial powers. Some are predominantly arguments about the nature of the actions in question: others are arguments about the meaning of the words conferring the powers. Clearly the contentions of Sir William Holdsworth and the majority

1. 58 *Law Quarterly Review* 2 (1942); cf. R. F. V. Heuston, 'Liversidge *v.* Anderson in Retrospect' 86 L.Q.R. 33 (1970) and 87 L.Q.R. 161 (1971).

judgments about such matters as the unsuitability of courts for judging issues requiring the assessment of confidential information would, if true, remain true no matter how explicitly the regulations had stated that the powers of the Minister were to be justiciable or reviewable. 'Justiciable' is in fact ambiguous. It could and sometimes does mean 'suitable [in the speaker's view] to determination by a court'. Alternatively, it may merely report the fact that an issue is one which has actually been given to the courts to decide. The distinction might be illustrated by a more recent episode—namely the decision in 1956 to transfer jurisdiction over restrictive practices in industry to a special division of the High Court. In the debates on the Restrictive Practices Bill it was argued against the Government's proposals that the question whether a restrictive practice was contrary to the public interest was not a justiciable issue but an administrative and political one. We cannot, one Opposition Member urged on that occasion, 'turn a political matter into a legal matter merely by asking the opinion of a judge about it'.[1] Nevertheless, if an issue is in fact handed over by Parliament for judicial determination the matter could be described as now 'justiciable'. Whether something is 'justiciable' in this sense is something which can only be determined by examining the terms of the law which bears on the matter. In 1942 Lord Atkin was prepared to hold that the words 'has reasonable cause' were clear enough to rule out the possibility of inferring from parliamentary or other circumstances that they were intended to be interpreted in a subjective sense. To argue against this conclusion simply on the ground that the Minister's conduct was of a kind which ought to be regarded as 'administrative' and 'not justiciable' could only be to beg the question as to the explicitness of the words. There are, it must be admitted, differences of opinion about the interpretation of statutes in situations where the apparent meaning of statutory words is in conflict with evidence about the actual views of the persons who enacted them. But it might be said in the *Liversidge* case first that there was no conclusive evidence that Parliament had any clear view upon the particular question (whatever opinions were held by the Minister, the law officers, or the draftsmen of the regulation), and secondly, that Lord Atkin's logic—if not his tact—seems to have been vindicated by subsequent events. In 1951 the Judicial Committee of the Privy Council suggested that the meaning of 'reasonable cause' allotted by the House of Lords in 1942 ought not to be regarded as laying down any general rule as to the construction of such phrases, and treated the words 'Where X has reasonable grounds to believe' as imposing a condition that there must in fact

1. 549 HC Deb., c. 2033 (6 March 1956).

exist reasonable grounds for the belief.[1] Moreover, when departments have wished to protect ministerial decisions from challenge in the courts they have not relied upon the 'reasonable cause' formula, but have adopted such phrases as 'if the Minister is satisfied', or 'if it appears necessary to the Minister'.

References to the responsibility of Ministers to Parliament, and to the responsibility of Parliament for controlling the discretion of Ministers, have occurred fairly indiscriminately in two rather different classes of dispute. The first is where a Minister or his department have been empowered to act for some general purpose. Where, for example, requisitioning powers had been granted by a Defence Regulation to maintain supplies and services essential to the life of the community, the Scottish Court of Session held that whether a particular service was in fact essential to the life of the community was 'a political question and . . . the exercise by the competent authority of a discretion in deciding it may be controlled by Parliament but cannot be reviewed in a court of law'.[2] Where powers are granted in peacetime to a department or to an independent board or corporation to pursue some generally defined purpose, it does not seem that any such confident conclusion can be drawn either from general considerations or from the presumption of parliamentary intention. It is not incompatible with the existence of parliamentary control for a judicial challenge to be possible at least on the grounds that powers have been used for some completely extraneous purpose or exercised in bad faith. Under the Electricity Act of 1947, for example, the Authority's duty is 'to develop and maintain an efficient, co-ordinated, and economical system of electricity supply' and the Boards are given power 'to do *anything* . . . which in their opinion is calculated to facilitate the proper performance of their duties'. This subjective discretion would not (to take an absurd example) permit the Authority to levy fines on wasteful consumers. Parliament must have intended —even if it did not clearly say—that the nationalised industries were to operate within their statutory jurisdiction and that the courts could keep them within it.[3]

The second class of cases in which references to the parliamentary function occur is that (met with in *Arlidge's*[4] case) where departments are acting in some sense as an umpire between a private individual and someone, either in a local authority or in the department itself, who has decided an issue against the individual. The compulsory

1. *Nakkuda Ali v. Jayaratne* [1951] AC 66.
2. *Pollock School v. Glasgow Town Clerk* [1946] SC 373, 387.
3. cf. *Anisminic v. Foreign Compensation Commission* [1969] 2 AC 147.
4. [1915] AC 120.

purchase, clearance, or designation of land by local authorities and Government departments provides the majority of examples. In reaching a final decision after considering the evidence of a public inquiry required under housing, acquisition of land, and town planning legislation, the Minister is not required to act as a judge. His conduct need not conform to the requirements of natural justice as interpreted by the courts, but only to the requirement of the legislature. 'No doubt Parliament always intends that a Minister should act reasonably', but 'justification if it is to be called for must be called for by Parliament'.[1] The part played by Parliament when the courts have considered these cases is an odd one. The fact that the Minister's exercise of his powers can be inquired into in the course of parliamentary debate and question, though it may be used to weigh down the scales of argument, does not usually play any central part and is rarely examined or evaluated. In *Arlidge's* case the appellant was turned away with the statement that departments were not bound to behave as courts. It was added that a single adjudicator could not decide all questions personally; that there was no power to administer an oath; and that inspectors' reports were confidential as being part of the department's documents in the same sense as its private minutes. In later cases other considerations based upon the nature of administrative procedures have been adduced. Public inquiries for example could be considered as 'informative' or as designed 'to elucidate matters upon which the Minister desires to be better informed',[2] rather than as judicial proceedings. Ministers could not be expected to have no departmental bias where action was initiated (as in designating the site of a new town) by the department itself.[3] Decisions might involve consultation with other departments whose views on policy a Minister was not bound to disclose. All these are considerations which are self-supporting and whose forcefulness would be not noticeably less if Parliament had no hand in the process at all (if for example Government departments were as constitutionally free from legislative control as American regulatory commissions).

Occasionally, however, judicial reasoning contains more explicit references to the parliamentary process than are involved in general remarks about the political answerability of Ministers. Inferences may, for example, be drawn from the fact that departmental regulations are generally required to be laid before one or both Houses. The conclusion that delegated legislative powers exercised by Mini-

1. *Robinson v. Minister of Town and Country Planning* [1947] KB 702, 717, 723.
2. ibid.
3. *Franklin v. Minister of Town and Country Planning* [1948] AC 87 at 102.

sters cannot be attacked in the courts on the ground of their unreasonableness, whilst bylaws made by local authorities can be so attacked, appears to be based (perhaps unreasonably) upon the appearance of ministerial rules on the table of the House. Again in 1950, the Court of Session was prepared to conclude from the provision that a draft scheme should be laid before each House before coming into operation that 'Parliament has not delegated to the Secretary of State, but expressly reserved to itself the final decision'.[1] But with what degree of seriousness can it be said that Parliament 'decides' something by providing for a departmental scheme or regulation to lie on the table of the House to await a possible prayer for its annulment within forty days? Despite the existence of the Commons Committee on Statutory Instruments, can it, in any but an artificial sense, be said that Parliament has reserved a final decision to itself by enacting that ministerial orders shall be laid in this way as the great majority are? The inference is perhaps more justifiable when orders are made subject to affirmative resolution and do not come into operation until debated and approved by resolution of the House. But for substantial conclusions to be based on 'parliamentary approval' the reality of the phrase in its various senses and the actual therapeutic value of the different forms of confirmation which lie behind it ought to have received more detailed judicial attention.

2. *Judicial control and the parliamentary process*

The Minister's responsibilities in relation to decisions which Parliament has delegated by statute vary considerably both in actual fact and in legal description. A Minister (or his department) may on different occasions be legislating on their own initiative, confirming a plan drawn up by a local authority, considering an appeal from a departmental or local decision, or approving a decision reached by an independent statutory body. In some of these roles a Minister's legal duties may differ from those imposed upon him in others. Even in the course of reaching a decision in a single case a Minister may have different capacities and, as it were, assume, doff, and reassume a number of different hats. The judicial hat (a somewhat doubtful and evanescent article) makes a fleeting appearance from time to time. In hearing objections through the medium of a public inquiry before confirming a compulsory purchase order under the Housing Acts the Minister of Health's functions were said by Lord Greene, Master of the Rolls, in 1947 to be administrative ones, 'but at a particular stage and for a particular and limited purpose, there is

1. *Magistrates of Ayr v. Lord Advocate* [1950] SC 102 at 107.

superimposed on his administrative character a character which is loosely described as quasi-judicial. . . . The administrative character in which he acts appears at a later stage.'[1]

Both when Ministers are acting in an appeal or adjudicatory capacity and when a Minister and his department are acting in effect as part of the legislative process there are two constitutional principles which may conflict with each other—or at least appear to do so. One of them is that the courts are the guardians of legality and private rights; the other that the responsibilities of Ministers and the privileges of the legislature must not be invaded or compromised. An apt illustration was provided in 1954. In December of that year there occurred what one Member of Parliament described in the House (doubtless with some exaggeration) as 'the most serious constitutional crisis since the reign of Queen Anne'.[2] The event in question was a High Court injunction restraining a Minister of the Crown—the Home Secretary—from submitting Orders approved by both Houses to the Queen for Assent in Council. The episodes which followed this action provoked a discussion in unusually dramatic terms of the relation of the courts to the administrative and parliamentary process.

The controversial Orders were laid by the Home Secretary to make a number of changes in constituency boundaries on the basis of reports submitted by the Parliamentary Boundaries Commissions.[3] The Minister's duty was to consider the recommendations and to lay them, with or without modification, before Parliament as draft Orders in Council. The proposals were opposed in many localities and legal action was begun to establish that the rules for reapportioning constituencies, laid down in the Act of 1949, had not been correctly applied by the Commissioners and that the Orders made by the Minister were consequently invalid.

The Borough Councils of Hammersmith and Fulham were first in the field, with an application for a mandatory injunction against the Boundary Commissioners themselves, requiring them to inform the Minister that the constituency proposals were *ultra vires*. In the Chancery Division of the High Court Mr Justice Harman refused to grant the injunction on the ground that the matter was not one for the intervention of the courts. His words as reported in *The Times* were that: 'Parliament could do anything. In this Act, it had provided

1. *B. Johnson and Co. (Builders) Ltd. v. Minister of Health* [1947] 2 All ER 395 at 399.
2. 535 HC Deb., 5s., c. 2453 (Mr Hale).
3. Under the House of Commons (Redistribution of Seats) Acts of 1944 and 1949. These provisions were amended in 1958.

itself with a staff to lean on in the form of the Boundary Commission. . . . Even though the Commission had misunderstood their functions by misreading the rules and thereby vitiating their report, Parliament could overlook the omission if it liked, being omnipotent, and make the resolution law. . . . It was said that the aggrieved had no method of voicing their grievance. His Lordship did not accept that. They were represented in Parliament like other citizens and could air their grievances there if they saw fit. . . . If there was justice in what they said, due weight would be given to it. A debate of this kind was entirely unsuited to judicial intervention.'[1]

A different view, however, was taken by Mr Justice Roxburgh. After the Commons had already taken note of, and approved, a number of the Home Secretary's Orders, a second action was brought by the Lord Mayor of Manchester for a declaration that the report relating to Manchester, Oldham, and Ashton under Lyne was not a report within the meaning of the Act, and could not properly be embodied in an Order to be submitted to Her Majesty in Council. On the basis of this *ex parte* application, Mr Justice Roxburgh granted an interim injunction restraining the Home Secretary from submitting the draft Order approved by the Commons for the Royal Assent. He noted that for the plaintiffs it was 'now or never'. If the draft Order in Council were submitted to the Queen it could not (by the terms of the parent Act) be called in question in the courts. From this fact (he went on) certain conclusions might be derived. One was that it was contemplated that the procedure would be subject to the jurisdiction of the courts until Her Majesty had made an Order in Council. (Here the argument makes an interesting comparison with that of Mr Justice Harman in the earlier case.) Nobody doubted, Mr Justice Roxburgh went on, that Parliament was supreme and that Parliament could repeal or enact any law, but it could only do that by passing enactments. This was a species of delegated legislation and it appeared from the form of the Act that it was intended that the courts should intervene in a proper case up to the time when Her Majesty made an Order in Council. It seemed to him (his Lordship) that the Secretary of State was not entitled to do anything unless and until the Boundary Commission had submitted a report under the Act, and he did not think that that entitled them to submit any kind of a report, but one in compliance with the Act. If he arrived at the conclusion that the report was not made in compliance with the Act, it would not be a proper draft for the Secretary of State to lay before Her Majesty, and it would not be affected by the resolutions of the

1. *Hammersmith Borough Council and Others v. Boundary Commission for England and Wales* (*Times* Law Report, 15.12.54).

two Houses. If anyone had intervened at an early stage (i.e. before the Order came up for debate), it might have been possible to prevent the Secretary of State from laying the Report before Parliament, but fortunately that opportunity was a thing of the past as the debate had taken place, and he (his Lordship) did not think that he was now in danger of running into conflict with parliamentary procedure.

The interim injunction did in fact impinge immediately upon parliamentary procedure. The Speaker ruled on 20 December that the House would not be debarred from continuing its discussions of the Orders not yet debated, by a decision that the reports were *ultra vires*. It was decided, however, that the remaining Orders would not be proceeded with until the legal position had been clarified and that no steps would be taken to submit to the Queen-in-Council the Orders already approved. Nevertheless the Government did not, in the words of the Leader of the House, accept the view that the matter was a justiciable one, rather than a matter to be decided by Parliament itself.[1] This argument was put before the Court of Appeal on the same day by the Attorney-General. To what extent it was upheld is not altogether easy to say. The Court (consisting of Lord Evershed and Lords Justices Jenkins and Hodson) set aside the *ex parte* injunction granted in the lower court on the ground that the Commissioners' reports were not in fact based upon a misinterpretation of the Redistribution of Seats Act. In the course of the judgment, however, Lord Evershed expressed in passing what seems to be a clear disagreement with the view of Mr Justice Roxburgh. Parliament, he thought, could always modify the Commission's recommendations. If the Commission were completely to disregard the provision of the Act of 1949, it was difficult to think that Parliament would pass such provisions by unnoticed. But if Parliament adopted them, it was unnecessary to say what view the Court might take. The case, he thought, 'was a striking one, coming near to touching on the privileges and powers of Parliament'.[2]

A similar, perhaps even more serious, view of the litigation in these cases was taken by some Members both of the Government and Opposition. On the day on which the Court of Appeal discharged the injunction against the Home Secretary, Mr Leslie Hale followed his remarks about 'the constitutional crisis' by saying that: 'For the first time in our Parliamentary history the courts have provisionally . . . asserted the right to interfere at the point when both Houses of

1. 535 HC Deb., 5s., c. 2447 (20 December 1954).

2. *Harper v. Secretary of State for the Home Department* [1955] 1 All ER 331 at 335.

Parliament have passed a measure, when although the formal consent of the Privy Council has technically to be obtained, we are in the position in which the royal assent has to be given. We are therefore bringing the matter of the veto of the Crown into question in the courts.'[1] A similar view was expressed in the Court of Appeal by the Attorney-General. There was, he argued, no right to intervene once the approval of both Houses had been obtained, and the injunction was in substance an injunction directed to the Crown, since it sought to restrain the submission of the draft Order to Her Majesty, so as to prevent her from considering whether to make the Order. Mr Paget, on the following day, when the injunction had been disposed of, thought that the constitutional position still remained undecided. 'The proposition,' he said, 'amounts to this: that the courts claim—and it has not been decided one way or the other whether this is a valid claim—that they have a right to deny to a Minister of the Crown access to the Crown. That seems to me to be an entirely novel claim by the courts and one of enormous constitutional importance. . . . Either by legislation or by some other means, ought not something to be done to clear up this very grave situation?'[2] Mr Silverman thought that a claim had been asserted which contained the seeds of 'a most undesirable conflict between Parliament and the courts',[3] and the Leader of the House, agreeing with Mr Paget's diagnosis of the situation, hoped that the Government would carry the House with it in the opinion that these were 'grave matters involving its rights' and not justiciable in the courts.[4] Political commentators outside were equally quick to denounce the threat of judicial encroachment. 'To give the judiciary power to interfere', wrote the *New Statesman* on 1 January 1955, 'is either to assume a fundamental law—such as the American Constitution—or to admit that the administrative and legislative functions of Parliament can be chopped into distinct parcels. Both concepts are alien to a Sovereign Parliament; and judicial review is the last doctrine that the Labour Party should champion.'

Yet such fears about the importation of the un-English concept of judicial review are surely misconceived. Statutory Orders in Council, despite their relative solemnity and submission to the Queen-in-Council, are still instruments of delegated legislation whose status is no higher than any other departmental order, and a legal challenge to the validity of delegated legislation has never been regarded as an

1. 535 HC Deb., 5s., c. 2453 (20 December 1954).
2. 535 HC Deb., 5s., c. 2607 (21 December 1954).
3. ibid., c. 2606.
4. ibid., c. 2603.

interference with the dignity or privileges of Parliament. Moreover, in speaking of a 'conflict between Parliament and the courts' there is a tendency to slide from the idea of 'Parliament', in the sense of the Commons or each House separately, to that of 'Parliament' in the full constitutional sense of Queen, Lords, and Commons in its sovereign capacity. In the *Hammersmith* case, for example, it was said that the Court should not substitute its judgment for that of the House of Commons and of the Lords. But the expressed reason was that 'Parliament' could overlook any defect, 'being omnipotent'. But resolutions of the Houses are not the action of 'the Queen-in-Parliament',[1] and Parliament's legal omnicompetence cannot properly be prayed in aid to cover the actions of one or both Houses when acting, not as the sovereign legislator, but as part of the mechanism of delegated legislation. Even when both Houses have approved a ministerial Order, the courts would retain a power to invalidate it if it could be shown to be beyond the powers granted in the parent Act. It is true that in this case the Orders in Council, when assented to in Council, were excluded by the parent Act[2] from judicial scrutiny, but this result followed from the legislative command of the Queen-in-Parliament expressed in the earlier Act and not from the resolution of each House in approving the Orders. In the absence of any such excluding section Orders in Council remain open to attack in the courts even after the Royal Assent has been given and despite their 'parliamentary' (in this sense of 'parliamentary') approval. It would seem, despite what was said in the Court of Appeal and in the Commons after the decision in *Harper's* case, that there must be limits to the extent to which defective ministerial Orders may be validated. During debate in the House the Speaker stated that if the House agreed to the Orders 'any defect . . . is cured, because nothing is *ultra vires* this House'.[3] The claim is certainly overstated. Though both the Minister and the House might modify an Order, such modification could hardly go outside the scheme of the parent Act. At any rate the legal supremacy of Parliament is not in itself an adequate foundation for a claim to exclusive jurisdiction by the Commons. In the face of a similar claim some years ago Lord Justice Younger remarked that 'The interference of the Court . . . so far from being even in the most diluted sense of the words a challenge to its supremacy, will be an assistance to Parliament.' In that case an application for *certiorari* was made to quash a scheme formulated by

1. *Stockdale v. Hansard* [1839] 9 Ad. & El. *Bowles v. Bank of England* [1913] 1, ch. 57.
2. Section 3 (7) of the Redistribution of Seats Act, 1949.
3. 535 HC Deb., 5s., c. 1919.

the Electricity Commissioners which required to be confirmed by parliamentary resolution. It was suggested, however, that the whole process was under the control of Parliament, which could (as with the Boundary Commissioners) modify the recommendations presented to it if it wished. The proceedings, it was argued, were part of the process by which Parliament was expressing its will, and judicial interference would be a trespass on the domain of the legislature. On this point Lord Justice Atkin said: 'It is unnecessary to emphasise the constitutional importance of this contention. Given its full effect it means that . . . new and onerous and inconsistent obligations [can be] imposed without an Act of Parliament and by simple resolution of both Houses of Parliament.'[1] In issuing a writ of prohibition: 'So far from seeking to diminish the authority of Parliament, we are performing the ordinary duty of the courts in upholding the enactments which it has passed.'[2]

Orders of *certiorari* and prohibition, however, can only be used to control schemes or decisions of a tribunal or commission acting judicially. A Minister given statutory discretion to adopt their findings is not acting in a judicial capacity and cannot be restrained in this way. Nor (it is now clear) can a Minister be restrained by an injunction from advising the Queen to assent to an invalid order, or from placing such an order before Parliament. An injunction will not, by the terms of the Crown Proceedings Act, lie against a Minister when he is acting as a servant of the Crown. Though it is artificial in the extreme to regard departmental legislation by Order in Council as a process in which the Queen considers what is proposed and takes advice before deciding to assent to it, nevertheless, in form that is what is being done when ministerial Orders are submitted, and the Minister can say with some degree of plausibility that he is acting in the capacity of Crown servant. In 1954 it was convincingly argued that he was not so acting when fulfilling a statutory obligation to place orders before the House. In the High Court hearing of *Harper's* case it was accepted that a Minister's statutory duties could be separated from his general duties as Secretary of State. Unfortunately the Court of Appeal has rejected that conclusion,[3] and refused to dissect the Minister. But despite these procedural difficulties (and a declaratory order would not be barred by the Crown Proceedings Act) two fairly simple conclusions can be drawn from these somewhat complex proceedings. The first is that a clear distinction is possible and necessary between the authority of Parliament and the

1. *R. v. Electricity Commissioners* [1924] 1 KB 171, 207, 208.
2. ibid. at p. 210.
3. cf. *Merricks v. Heathcoat-Amory* [1955] 2 All ER 453 at 456.

subordinate functions of the Houses when acting with Ministers as a part of the mechanism of delegated legislation. The second conclusion is that parliamentary authority or control ought not to be regarded as in any way analogous to, or as a substitute for, judicial control where questions involving the impartial interpretation of statutory provisions are raised.

The deficiencies of the legislature as an alternative organ of control were, in fact, well illustrated by the Boundary Commission debates of 1954–5. The practical failings of Parliament as it sometimes appears in the judicial eye—in a shape not far removed from its traditional description as 'the grand inquest of the nation'—were fully revealed in the process. The difference between the role for which Parliament had been cast by the Court of Appeal and that which Members found themselves playing was keenly felt on both sides of the House. On the day following the *Hammersmith* case, Mr Michael Stewart said: 'I should like very briefly to refer to the case in the courts yesterday. The judge in that case . . . took the view that he could not intervene because it was possible for this House to intervene. He said that the persons who had a grievance . . . "were represented in Parliament like other citizens and could air their grievances there . . ."—always provided that they are lucky enough to catch your eye, Mr Speaker—"and if there was justice in what they said, due weight would be given to it." The learned judge is not acquainted with the operation of three-line Whips.'[1] The Government's decision to debate the Orders with the Whips on raised a dilemma which was pointed out continuously by speakers opposing the Orders. Any errors of law or policy, the courts had said, could be put right by the Minister and by Parliament. Though the Minister, in presenting his Orders, remarked that Parliament could do what it liked with the recommendations and that it was for the House to decide what course to take, speakers of all parties continuously lamented that this was exactly what the House could not do. For a number of local authorities, one Member argued, the House was their only court of appeal. But as another backbencher (Mr Silverman) urged, the House could not play that part, or participate in the administrative process in a judicial way, in the absence of a free vote. They could not be judicial under a three-line Whip. He had never 'regarded a Whip as a judicial instrument'.[2] This topic, however, the Speaker ruled to be out of order. 'I know,' he said, 'nothing about Whips.'[3]

1. 535 HC Deb., 5s., c. 1844 (15 December 1954).
2. 535 HC Deb., 5s., c. 2059.
3. ibid., c. 1924. Whips now appear in Erskine-May, though (18th ed., 1971, p. 239).

The corresponding judicial myopia has had in this sphere a not dissimilar consequence. A major component of post-war disquiet about governmental discretion was undoubtedly the growing awareness (in all political parties) that a potential absence of control might lurk behind an artificial phraseology about parliamentary redress and an allocation to the legislature of a role which it does not and cannot play. In the absence of confidence in the judiciary[1] as protectors of citizens' rights it was inevitable that in the 1950s and 60s thoughts should turn to alternative possibilities for securing justice for complainants against the administration.

1. It now seems that this judgment may have been too pessimistic. Since about 1964 the House of Lords has in a number of decisions displayed what seems to be a robuster attitude to ministerial and administrative discretion. A particularly striking example was *Padfield v. Minister of Agriculture, Fisheries and Food* [1968] AC 997, in which mandamus issued to control what appeared to be on its face an unfettered discretion. The relevant Act contained a power framed in subjective terms ('If the Minister so directs'), but it was held that 'Parliament must have conferred the discretion with the intention that it should be used to promote the policy and objects of the Act'. cf. the *Anisminic* case (p. 71 n.3 above).

6

ADMINISTRATIVE JUSTICE

1. *The growth of administrative powers*

To glance through the chapter headings of Bagehot's *English Constitution* is to realise how the centre of gravity in matters of government has altered since the latter half of the nineteenth century. Bagehot was concerned with events occurring mostly within the confines of Westminster, Windsor, and Whitehall. Today books about the Constitution occupy themselves with a number of other topics and they are as likely to be concerned with local government or administrative tribunals as with the Queen. Sir Kenneth Wheare's *Government by Committee*, for example, is not inaptly sub-titled *An Essay on the British Constitution*—and is devoted to an analysis of the function of committees in local and central administration. Professor W. A. Robson's *Justice and Administrative Law* has a similar sub-title. It is noteworthy that much of this constitutional machinery of administration, negotiation, and consultation which has grown up in the inter-war, second war, and post-war periods is unknown even to those who are relatively literate in public matters. How many, for example, could claim easy familiarity with the doings of (say) the National Housing and Town Planning Council, the Advisory Committee on Sand and Gravel, or the United Chamois Leather Layers Out Society (names picked at random from *Government by Committee*)? Yet bodies such as these and hundreds like them[1] play a necessary part in the machinery of government. In 1872, or even 1914, nobody would have thought that gravel, or chamois leathers, or town plan-

1. Some information as to the number may be gathered from the following exchange in the House in December 1958. Mr Lipton asked the Chancellor of the Exchequer how many advisory boards advised Her Majesty's Government at national level.

Mr Simon (Financial Secretary, Treasury): There are about 850 advisory bodies of a central or national character. (Laughter.)

Mr Lipton: With this wealth of advice available to the Government, how is it that they get into such a frightful mess?

ning, had anything to do with government, and every educated layman knew that the elements of the Constitution were the Queen, Ministers, and both Houses of Parliament.

In this sphere of central government at least, Bagehot and Dicey between them provided many of the starting points and much of the vocabulary of British political studies. In a sense neither of them is out of date. Their exposition of the principles of Cabinet Government, of the authority of Parliament, of the Rule of Law and of the constitutional conventions still provides a necessary introduction to the understanding of our governmental system. These principles are, in one sense, all we have in the way of fundamental constitutional tenets. But undoubtedly circumstances have changed a great deal in the present century. Perhaps the most striking evidences of change are the multiplication of administrative bodies created by statute and the increasing part played by legislative activity in general. Bagehot listed legislation last in his analysis of the functions of Parliament. 'Generally,' he thought, 'the laws of a nation suit its life; special adaptations of them are but subordinate.' Now we consider the discussion of legislation the first and natural function of Parliament. The 1912 edition of Grant Robertson's *Select Statutes and Documents* does not include a single Act of Parliament passed in the second half of the nineteenth century. The only piece of parliamentary handiwork found worthy of notice between the Reform Act of 1832 and the Parliament Act of 1911 is the Abolition of Slavery Act of 1833. The legislative activity of the twentieth century stands in sharp contrast. Of statues passed since 1900 probably a majority are enactments which either create new statutory bodies or confer powers of regulation on existing authorities, and they are concerned with such matters as Trade Unions, Rating and Valuation, Housing, Education, Health, Gas and Coal. This development is of course familiar in all western and Commonwealth countries, and it has been the staple diet of social historians, economists, and party politicians. But its influence on constitutional as distinct from political and economic ideas has probably been less marked in this country than on the Continent. The French jurist, Léon Duguit, for example, early in the present century was insisting that the new functions performed by the State and Government had made them the 'managers of the nation's business'.[1] This doctrine was asserted to be an alternative to the conception of the state as an entity exercising 'sovereign' power over its citizens, and it suggested a theoretical basis upon which a system of governmental responsibility for the consequences to individuals of official action might be elaborated. In this country we have

1. *Law and the Modern State* (transl. Laski 1921), p. 51.

never had a theory of the state and, as the legal historian, Frederick Maitland, observed, we are gradually getting into trouble for it. ('There is wonderfully little of the State in Blackstone's *Commentaries*.'[1]) As Maitland noted, the law of England has used the King's authority as a substitute for such a theory. The legal doctrine which the textbook writers found in Blackstone declared executive power to be vested in the King, who in his 'politic' capacity could do no wrong, nor (according to Blackstone) even think it. Dicey made fun of Blackstone for omitting to make plain the extent to which the legal theory was modified by constitutional practice. (One of Dicey's reasons for this seems to have been that literal-minded law students, wedded to their Blackstone, might be deceived into thinking that the Queen spent her time imprisoning felons and collecting taxes.) But Maitland observed also that besides being untrue as a statement of constitutional fact the doctrine was no longer true even as law. Executive powers were, he remarked, frequently conferred by Parliament directly on departments and public bodies. The executive power of the nation was no longer, even legally, an exclusive possession of the Crown.

Today, the question whether powers are exercised in name by the Queen through her Ministers, or by Ministers acting under powers devolved directly on them by statute, is purely a formal one and is decided by Ministers in any case. A distinction of somewhat greater importance is between decisions made by formal parliamentary enactment after readings in each House and those which are made by Departmental Civil Servants under discretionary authority delegated to them by statute. When the growth of delegated power of this latter kind began to attract public comment, after the First World War, it was perhaps significant testimony to the impact of Dicey's two principles, the Supremacy of Parliament and the Rule of Law, that they should have been stated as the obvious criteria of healthy government —for example in the terms of reference of the Donoughmore Committee, which reported on the exercise of Ministers' Powers in 1932. The Committee's conclusion was that both principles remained intact, and this in its way was, and is, almost bound to be true. The authority for official actions is still contained in Acts of Parliament, and penalties are still imposed in the last resort by judges and policemen, applying known legal rules in a consistent manner. There is probably no reasonably conceivable governmental action in this country, outside of a revolutionary situation, which we should be willing to count as a clear negation of the rule of law or the sovereignty of Parliament. Nevertheless, it was undeniable that the discretionary power which

1. 'The Crown as Corporation', *Selected Essays* (1936), p. 112.

Dicey condemned as inimical to the rule of law had leaked into the twentieth-century system in fairly large amounts.

The technicality of social and economic legislation, and the conferring on Government departments of powers to make rules and decide disputes, have combined to present an entirely new problem of control which the Constitution in Dicey's day saw only in its beginning. In this country the mechanisms for the control of power have traditionally been twofold: first the sanctions of the civil and criminal law applied by the law courts, and secondly the control, exercised, as Burke said, on behalf of the people, of the High Court of Parliament. The distinction between the two methods of control is, at least in principle, fairly clear. The function of parliamentary debate is to air grievances against the policy and proposals of Her Majesty's Government, and if possible to get Her Majesty's Ministers to change their minds. It is an argumentative process, rather than a judicial one. The function of the courts, on the other hand, is predominantly that of providing remedies for individuals against unlawful damage inflicted on them by other individuals, and the process is surrounded by strict rules of procedure and evidence. The extension of State activity and the growth of different kinds of 'damage' to individual interests have destroyed the simplicity of this distinction. A good many recent constitutional disagreements boil down to the question whether a particular type of damage or dispute falls into the area where control ought to be exercised (if at all) by parliamentary means, into that where it ought to be exercised by judicial means, or into some disputed middle ground uneasily and increasingly overcrowded by disputes between private individuals and bodies which are agents (in some sense) of Government and Administration. It must be conceded further that a fair generalisation about the history in this country of individual efforts to attack the exercise of administrative powers in the courts would be that it is a record of comparative failure. In this narrative, Parliament and its legislation must take the major share of credit or blame and the doctrine of ministerial responsibility to Parliament may be cast for the role of either hero or villain according to the importance attached to administrative freedom.

The tension between the rights of the individual and the freedom of government departments to administer the law, and to act according to their own notions of fair procedure, was already a topic of academic discussion before Dicey's death. In 1915 Dicey wrote an article in the *Law Quarterly Review* entitled 'The Development of Administrative Law in England'. The term 'administrative law' itself had already acquired an alien odour (from which it is still not free) largely because of Dicey's own strictures upon *droit administratif*—by which he meant the French system of special courts for the settlement of administrative disputes, exercising a parallel jurisdiction to the ordinary civil criminal courts. The English term, as used for example in the writing of John Austin earlier in the nineteenth century, had been innocent of any such implication of special administrative jurisdiction or privilege, and had meant simply the general law of the land governing the exercise of the Sovereign's powers either by the Sovereign or subordinate authorities. This is admittedly a wide definition and one practically identical with constitutional law; but in his article of 1915 Dicey was using the term in this sense to signify the extension of powers by the ordinary law of the land to agents of the Government who were yet subject to the control of the ordinary law courts. What was in issue was the extent of this control and the degree to which the statutes regulating the conduct of the newer administrative bodies gave them a discretion to make decisions affecting the legal rights, and particularly the property rights, of individuals in accordance with procedures which differed from those of courts of law. Dicey, whatever his attitude to *droit administratif*, was prepared to concede the necessity of this development. He agreed that the management of the business of a government department was not the same thing as the conduct of a trial in a court of law. He was commenting here on a decision of the House of Lords which had just held (in *Local Government Board v. Arlidge*)[1] that the Board was not compelled to follow the procedure of a court of law in dealing with an objection to the imposition of a closing order on a house in Hampstead, under the provisions of the Housing and Town Planning Act of 1909. Arlidge, the objector, claimed that the procedure of the Board was contrary to natural justice since he had not been heard personally by whoever had decided against his objection and had not been allowed to see the report of the Board's inspector. Though Arlidge was upheld in the Court of Appeal, the House of Lords held that Parliament had intended the department to follow its own procedure, and that provided appeals were dealt with fairly and without bias, and that opportunity to present a case was given to an objector, there was no obligation to follow the procedural rules necessary to a hearing in a court of law. 'The only authority that can review what has been done,' said Viscount Haldane, 'is Parliament, to which the Minister in charge is responsible.' That sentiment was often to be repeated.

Dicey, none the less, remained optimistic about the guarantees provided by the common law. 'In some form or other,' he thought,

1. [1915] AC 120.

'the English courts will always find the means for correcting the injustice, if demonstrated, of any exercise, by a Government Department of judicial or quasi-judicial authority.'[1] On the whole, and perhaps until rather recent times, Dicey's fellow lawyers have contrived fairly successfully to avoid so sanguine a conviction. It has been a commonly expressed belief that the decay of judicial resistance to the claims of the executive began with *Arlidge's* case. It was, Sir Carleton Allen has argued, 'an opportunity for the House of Lords to place much of our administrative law on a sound basis—an opportunity not only lost but thrown away with both hands'.[2] Professor C. J. Hamson, in his study of the French Conseil d'État, has added that, had Dicey 'lived to observe the extent to which the High Court has abdicated from its jurisdiction, he would, I have no doubt, have preferred today the French result'.[3] Neither writer could be accused of ignoring the constraining effects on the judiciary of legislation by Parliament; but expressions such as 'opportunity', and 'abdicate' do at least tend to suggest that judges have regulated or refrained from regulating the activities of government departments chiefly in response to the strength of their personal convictions about the desirable limits of such activities. Such a conclusion could only be safely arrived at after fairly extensive psychological and sociological investigations, from which judges (at least on this side of the Atlantic) have, on the whole, remained immune. It is certainly true that the interpretation of statutes and the application of common law remedies inevitably permit a degree of judicial discretion. But the extent to which the admittedly increasing powers of the executive in the twentieth century reflect any genuine trend in judicial opinion about the merits of executive action, or any increased tolerance of it, is obviously complicated by the diligent application of a clear parliamentary intention to free administrative judgments about the public interest from judicial control.

2. *The 'public interest principle'*

That the 'public interest' is best judged by Ministers responsible to Parliament is of course the practical conclusion upon which British administrative procedures are founded. It is admirably summed up in the view that 'The Government must always get its own way if it thinks the matter is sufficiently important, or cease to be the Government: that is a shocking doctrine to Americans and Frenchmen and

1. (1915) 31, *Law Quarterly Review* at 151.
2. *Law and Orders* (2nd ed.), p. 278 n.
3. *Executive Discretion and Judicial Control* (1954), p. 52.

their camp-followers, but it happens to be our system.'[1] To assiduous opponents of bureaucracy who have turned envious eyes to the judicial remedies available against government in the United States, or to the extensive inquisitory powers of the French Conseil d'État, there is an undoubtedly robust answer to hand in the contention that the status given to Ministers in the British Constitution, along with the rejection of the separation of powers doctrine, is incompatible with any such alien pattern of judicial control, and that adequate substitutes exist in the presence of departmental heads in the legislature and the practice of the parliamentary question. But this answer is too robust if it precludes any discussion of the public interest principle itself. The principle is not, on a closer view, one without admitted exceptions. If it were rigorously asserted it might well lead to the view that wherever any governmental authority pursuing a public purpose is engaged in a dispute with a private individual, an administrator might justifiably decide the matter out of hand in all cases, since he is responsible to a Minister who is popularly elected and answerable to Parliament for the action of his officials. This view is not in fact taken, since it is thought to be right, in at least some cases, for a clash between a public and a private interest to be resolved by an independent decision (for example by a tribunal) which is binding on the Minister. The public interest is here expressed partly through a channel which is substantially independent of Ministers as far as individual disputes are concerned. One obvious corollary of departing from the public interest principle is that the ambit in which parliamentary questioning is possible is narrowed. This corollary was well recognised on both sides of the House when the Restrictive Trade Practices Act was passed in 1956, to provide for the creation of a Restrictive Practices Court. The Labour Party based its opposition to the Act largely on the ground that the control of all monopolistic practices should be retained exclusively by the Minister advised by an administrative body (such as the Monopolies Commission) and answerable to Parliament. To allow matters involving the public interest to be decided by a body not subject to parliamentary questioning was, it was contended, an abdication of responsibility by both the Government and the House. 'Once we have parted with the Bill,' said a Labour spokesman, 'we shall have parted with the control of the Restrictive Practices mentioned in it.' The Bill, he added, was handing over to an outside body governmental and parliamentary power.[2] The President of the Board of Trade agreed with this conclusion. He did not propose after the

1. R. M. Jackson, 'Ministerial Tribunals', *Manchester Guardian*, 22 April 1955.
2. 594 HC Deb., 5s., c. 2029 (Mr Ungoed-Thomas) (6 March 1956).

passing of the legislation to make governmental decisions on matters which were now made justiciable. To do so would bring about an intolerable conflict between Parliament and the new Restrictive Practices Court.

The Government, however, have clearly been prepared to face the shrinkage in the powers of inquisition exercised by the House in this field, as both major parties have been willing to face a similar restriction of parliamentary questioning in relation to decisions on administrative matters made by the Boards of Nationalised Industries. In sum, all that can be deduced from the public interest principle as at present applied is that where an issue is of such a kind that it ought to be resolved in a way that permits individual decisions to be questioned in Parliament, then the issue ought not to be made subject to an independent or judicial determination. But exactly what issues are of this kind is a matter which may vary considerably with the attitudes of Members and Ministers from time to time. Nor has the House been supplied with any persuasive general principles to help it decide what is possible and desirable. The advice given by the Committee of Ministers' Powers in 1932 was that 'a decision which ultimately turns on administrative policy should normally be taken by the executive Minister'.[1] But this is empty advice. Whether something 'ultimately' turns upon administrative policy depends upon Parliament. It is precisely what Parliament has to decide in legislating for an administrative solution or an independent arbitration, and the decision is not made easier by being told that decisions which should ultimately be made by Ministers ought to be made by Ministers.

3. *The influence of constitutional and political theories*

It is interesting to speculate why legal philosophy and constitutional theory have not thrown up in this country anything analogous to the body of thought which has underlain remedies against ministerial decisions in France and other continental jurisdictions. In such theories the view that the government must always get its way is seen in a different light, and the right of citizens to have an independent judgment in disputes between themselves and the government is merely part of a theory in which both government and citizens are each elements in a wider organism. The doctrine of political pluralism is perhaps the nearest theoretical counterpart in this country. Harold Laski's attacks on the sovereignty of the state, in the sense of the legal immunities of the Crown, corresponded in some measure to the legal theory advanced in France by Duguit (whom Laski trans-

1. Cmnd. 4060 (1932), p. 93.

lated[1]). But though something might be made of the effect of political theory via Laski's presence on the Donoughmore Committee, the total impact of philosophical considerations upon administrative remedies in Britain cannot have been very great. Some have been inclined to lay the blame upon Dicey. It has been suggested that the result of his emphasis upon the sovereignty of Parliament has been a 'refusal to recognise the duality of the state, or to admit any distinction between sovereign and non-sovereign aspects'. Hence (it has been argued) there arises a doubt about 'the very existence or necessity of public law'.[2] This particular connection of ideas seems to involve a confusion between Dicey's legislative sovereignty and sovereignty in the sense of a freedom from legal controls of the *executive* organs of the state. Though Dicey's parliamentary sovereign is free from legal control in the sense of being able to repeal any law, there is nothing in his exposition of sovereignty which is incompatible with the sovereign Queen-in-Parliament imposing any rules of legal liability, however strict, upon the Crown or Government. Nevertheless, Dicey's general dislike of the divided jurisdiction entailed by the French *droit administratif* almost certainly influenced the thinking of common lawyers about administrative remedies. In the result we have seen in this country nothing in the way of abstract theorising about the nature of the state in its sovereign and non-sovereign characters. In its place there has been only a pragmatic and sometimes confused debate about the restriction of Crown privilege and the boundaries between judicial control and administrative discretion—a debate carried on for the most part in the courts, with academic lawyers, Parliamentary Select Committees, and (more lately) party political pamphleteers keeping the sidelines. Some rather broad—and perhaps misleading—trends in the argument became discernible in the nineteen-thirties. Criticism of judicial control of the administration was noticeably associated with radical political opinion. Sympathy with collectivist objectives tended to focus left-wing criticism upon any judicial determination whose result was to impede a useful administrative object. Harold Laski, in his note appended to the Donoughmore Report, wrote that the canons of interpretation applied by the courts enabled the judge 'to substitute his private notions of legislative intention for those which the authors of the statute sought to fulfil'. Judges, he urged, were insufficiently aware of 'what Mr Justice Holmes has called his "inarticulate major

1. *Law and the Modern State* (1921).
2. W. Friedmann, *Law and Social Change in Contemporary Britain* (1951), p. 178.

premiss" '.[1] The attitude towards judicial review on a wider scale in the United States throughout the thirties was also predominantly one of hostility on the part of political liberals. Right-wing political sympathies on the other hand have tended to cast the judiciary in the role of guardian for private rights of liberty and property. The seeds of potential confusion in these alignments ripened early in the United States, where opposition to judicial 'activism' is no longer a characteristic of the political left; and minor reflections of the same conflict of loyalties have in recent years been plain in this country. When the wielding of administrative power is in the hands of a Conservative administration, the attitudes of both right and left to judicial restraint may be affected. Adherents of each of the political parties have in relatively recent times produced manifestos about the control of ministerial powers which cannot be said to vary on serious matters of principle. The almost entirely beneficial result is that the principles involved in judicial interpretation, and proposals for appeals from departmental decisions, can now be discussed in a fairly non-partisan atmosphere.

4. *The Establishment view*

In any such debate in Great Britain proponents of any extension of external controls over the actions of Ministers and Civil Servants are faced with a set of built-in resistances in the constitutional system itself. Amongst them are the beliefs about its working which have accumulated within administrative circles, and which are inherited to some extent by successive incumbents irrespective of any political affiliation. One such structure of beliefs is that about the status of the Civil Service and its relations with Ministers. The principle that the Civil Service must be in a position to give anonymous and confidential advice to Ministers has been a powerful incentive to resist proposals which might open departmental files to outside scrutiny. The consistent willingness of departmental heads, of whatever political complexion, to continue to claim the Crown's privilege of refusing to disclose documents in the course of litigation has largely turned upon this point. As laid down by the House of Lords in 1942[2] the privilege rested upon two grounds—the potential danger to public security, and the proper functioning of the public service. Much criticism has been directed to the vagueness of the second category, and the Government in 1956 stated that departmental practice would be altered so as to avoid the claiming of privilege for certain minor categories of

1. Cmnd. 4060 (1932), p. 135.
2. *Duncan v. Cammell Laird* [1942] AC 624. The documents in this case related to the design of the submarine *Thetis*.

documents such as medical records of departmental employees, and the reports of departmental eyewitnesses in accidents involving government departments. But the Lord Chancellor speaking in the House of Lords said that privilege must be maintained over a wide area to secure 'freedom and candour of communication' within the public service. Where the legality of a Minister's actions was being challenged in the courts there would, he thought, be grave prejudice to the efficiency of administration if it were possible to secure disclosure of departmental and interdepartmental minutes. A plaintiff might seek to show that the Minister acted on wrong principles, by reference to the opinions expressed by individual Civil Servants during the process of discussion and advice prior to decision. Actions such as malicious prosecution, wrongful imprisonment, or defamation might be concerned with events of public interest giving rise to comment in the Press and questions in Parliament. If advice were to be given at a high level in such cases, it was necessary that it should be entirely frank and not subject to discovery in subsequent proceedings.[1] Fortunately, the courts have now rejected this view.[2]

It is of course merely a reformulation of the 'public interest principle' to hold that when anything arises which can be construed as raising a question of 'policy', nothing should be interposed, either between a Minister and his Civil Servants or between the Minister and Parliament (though it does not follow merely from this that nobody shall decide what is an issue of policy but a Minister). The principle is deep-rooted in ideas about British government and has been taken to imply that when Ministers answer for policy they must answer to the House as a whole and not to any other body even if that body be a committee of the House. When the Commons's Select Committee on Statutory Rules and Orders (now known as the Statutory Instruments Committee) was set up in 1944 to examine the subordinate rules and orders made by government departments, some doubt seems to have existed in the minds of members as to whether the Committee would be able to call Ministers before it. Mr Herbert Morrison's views on the question, however, were emphatic 'We do not think,' he said, 'that the Committee should have the power to send for Ministers. The place for Ministers to argue is at this Box, and moreover, subject to the House, they have to have the last word on the floor of the House if the matter comes to an issue. If they had been upstairs, everybody might be embarrassed.'[3] The function of the Committee, he added, was to protect the authority of

1. 197 HL Deb., cs. 741–7 (6 June 1956).
2. See *Conway v. Rimmer* [1968] AC 910.
3. 400 HC Deb., 5s., c. 269 (17 May 1944).

Parliament and it would be intolerable if questions involving the merits of what Parliament had enacted were to be redebated in the Select Committee. But if the purpose of the Committee is to protect the authority of Parliament against improper use of the powers delegated to departments (and therefore Ministers), it can hardly be assumed *a priori* that the merits of Parliament's policy are automatically embodied in the policy of the Ministers' regulations. Since one of the Committee's functions is to inquire into an 'unusual' or 'unexpected' use of powers delegated to the Minister, who better to ask for an explanation than the Minister himself? In the event, however, the Morrisonian view has governed the Committee's interpretation of its power to require a government department to 'explain' its legislative activity. The departmental witnesses whom it interrogates can explain what has been done but it is not thought to be within their province to explain, beyond a certain point, why it has been done. The Committee's primary function is of course—in the words of a former chairman (Mr Godfrey Nicholson)—'simply to show the red light to the House of Commons'. On one occasion when members of the Committee had been pressing witnesses as to the necessity for certain orders, the Chairman intervened with the ruling that 'This is a question of departmental administration. It seems to me that we must be careful how far we go. It is most interesting, but if the Ministry say that they wish to do a thing in a certain way it is not for us to check or to criticise it. Our only task is to satisfy ourselves that there is or is not a breach of recognised practice in the making or the laying of an order.'[1]

These principles were to some extent challenged in 1946 when Sir Gilbert Campion (as he then was) suggested in a memorandum to the Select Committee on the Procedure of the House that the House should delegate a part of its supervisory power to the Statutory Instruments Committee and explicitly extend its terms of reference to include consideration of the merits of departmental legislation 'from the point of view of its efficiency as a means of carrying out the purposes named by the Act'. The Committee might consider whether a ministerial order was 'well designed for its purpose and whether the method chosen was the least injurious to the rights of the citizen'. It might also undertake to investigate citizens' complaints about the working of delegated legislation.[2]

These questions were considered by the Committee on Procedure to be too wide for its consideration and it was recommended that

1. *Select Committee on Statutory Instruments*, Minutes of Evidence (23 July 1951), p. 3.
2. HC 189–1 (1946), pp. xi–xii.

the whole question of delegated legislation should be investigated by a further Select Committee. A memorandum submitted to the 1946 Committee by the Government repeated the arguments used by Mr Morrison in 1944. The extension of the Committee's field of inquiry, it was said, would give it access to all phases of government administration within the field covered by delegated powers, and Ministers would have to attend to defend their policy. Other witnesses argued that it would be impossible to separate the merits of regulations from those of the statute passed by Parliament and that complaints could not be investigated without going into departmental correspondence. Professor E. C. S. Wade in evidence submitted to the Committee also opposed the Campion plan but suggested in the alternative that there might be consultation on the merits of a departmental order with a committee or committees of the House before the order were made. The notion that consultation by Ministers with such committees undermined the Minister's responsibility was, Professor Wade suggested, plausible in matters of high policy but on more technical matters the detraction from ministerial responsibility would not, he believed, be a serious one. In the face of what might be called the Establishment view, Professor Wade's suggestion bore no more fruit than that of Lord Campion. A Committee was eventually set up in 1952 to examine delegated legislation.[1] Its report in the following year together with the declining annual output and the supervision of the Statutory Instruments Committee seem finally to have stilled disquiet about the legislative powers of the administration. Correspondingly, however, anxiety about governmental inquiry procedures appeared to increase. The proposals of reformers to separate those parts of administrative activity which might be called technical, or (more daringly by some) justiciable from inviolable ministerial policy, cut across not only the field of delegated legislative powers but also all the activities of government departments which had been called in the terms of reference of the Donoughmore Committee 'judicial' and 'quasi-judicial'. It is principally upon these powers that public criticisms of 'bureaucracy' has been focussed in the years since 1945. Since the Report of the Committee on Ministers' Powers a considerable extension has taken place in the number of disputes between public and private authority which are resolved either by administrative tribunals set up by departments to hear appeals against awards made under social service statutes (pensions, insurance, industrial injuries and so on) or by public inquiries held before the compulsory acquisition of land by local or governmental

1. HC 310 (1953).

authorities. Since the first half of the 1932 Committee's conclusions had been reviewed by the Select Committee on Delegated Legislation of 1952–3, it was appropriate that some inquiry should take place into the remainder of the conclusions arrived at twenty years earlier. Amidst the murmurings about administrative lawlessness which were the aftermath of the Crichel Down inquiry in 1954[1] the Government found itself caught between Opposition criticism on the one hand and, on the other, long-standing resentment amongst its supporters of the very existence of governmental control of private rights in land. The offspring of this somewhat oddly matched union of forces was the Franks Committee on Administrative Tribunals and Inquiries. The implicit major question into which Sir Oliver Franks and his colleagues, like their predecessors, were inquiring was the working of the public interest.

5. *The analysis of the Committee on Ministers' powers*

The Committee set up in 1929 under the chairmanship of the Earl of Donoughmore (later succeeded by Sir Leslie Scott) were commanded by their terms of reference to consider the powers exercised by Ministers and to report what safeguards were necessary to preserve the sovereignty of Parliament and the supremacy of the law. The threat to the former principle was implicitly contained in the practice of delegated legislation and to the latter principle in the exercise by departments of what the Committee called in the opening paragraphs of its Report 'powers of judicial or quasi-judicial decision'. In the second half of the Report these terms were defined in words which have provided the starting point of almost every subsequent discussion of administrative reform. A judicial decision, the Committee said, was an application of the law of the land to a dispute between two parties each presenting (though not necessarily orally) evidence as to the facts of the dispute and if necessary submissions of law. A quasi-judicial decision, on the other hand, was a decision in a dispute between parties which was reached in the last resort by the application of a Minister's policy to the facts of the case. Such a decision might in the preliminary stages involve a judicial element since before a Minister's administrative discretion could operate he might by statute be required to consider representations and ascertain the facts. But the final resolution was a matter of free choice, though one which, in the Committee's view, had to be 'actuated by the elementary principles of reason and justice'. A purely administrative decision was to be distinguished on the ground that it was an entirely different

1. *Public Inquiry into the Acquisition of Land at Crichel Down* (Cmnd. 9176, 1954).

mental act. A determination of the Admiralty, for example, to place a contract for stores was a determination to pursue a course of administrative conduct, but it was not a 'decision' in the sense that any dispute existed which had to be resolved by weighing submissions and collating evidence.

Despite an air of apparent clarity and decisiveness, the Committee's use of this vocabulary contains at least apparent inconsistencies. Sometimes, for example, in speaking of a Minister's action after the hearing of representations, the Report states that 'his ultimate decision is quasi-judicial'. On other occasions such action is said to be 'administrative'. 'Quasi-judicial', in other words, is applied ambiguously both to the whole process which contains a judicial element followed by a policy determination and to the ultimate policy determination itself, despite the fact that that determination is also spoken of as administrative action. Moreover, the difficulty of identifying the functions defined in these terms by the Committee has been fully demonstrated in the courts when the actions of Ministers under housing and town-planning legislation have been disputed. The case of *Franklin v. Minister of Town and Country Planning*[1] illustrates both this difficulty and the uncertainty of the advice proffered by the Donoughmore Committee. In that instance the Minister had made an order designating an area of land at Stevenage as the site of a new town, after considering the objections offered at a local public inquiry held by one of the Ministry's inspectors. The objectors applied to the High Court to quash the Minister's order on the ground that his publicly expressed political views about the necessity for placing the new town at Stevenage prevented him from fulfilling the quasi-judicial duty of considering the objections to the scheme with an open mind. This plea was first upheld in the High Court, but the decision was reversed in the Court of Appeal on the ground that the Minister had not in fact neglected to perform his quasi-judicial duties in an unbiassed way. On appeal to the House of Lords the objectors lost again on the ground that the Minister had no quasi-judicial duties to neglect, so that the question whether his mind was open or closed was immaterial, provided only that the objections had been heard and the inspector's report on them considered. 'No judicial or quasi-judicial duty,' said Lord Thankerton, 'was imposed on the Minister, and any reference to judicial duty or bias is irrelevant.' The Minister's duties were 'purely administrative'.[2] This is a use of 'administrative' which is clearly not quite what the Committee

1. [1948] AC 81.
2. [1948] AC 87 at 102.

on Ministers' Powers had in mind when it spoke of the administrative action of a department in placing a contract or arranging its own affairs and is more like the dispute resolved by an application of policy which the Committee called 'quasi-judicial'. The uncertainty infected the advice which the Committee gave in its Report. That advice was based upon two principles. The first was that statutes should provide for an independent decision by a tribunal or the courts where there might be a departmental interest in the outcome of a judicial decision. The second principle was that where decisions had to be made which turned upon administrative policy they should normally be made not by a tribunal but by a Minister. Both pieces of advice depend for their usefulness upon knowing precisely which decisions are to be counted as 'judicial' and which as 'administrative'.

The Committee on Ministers' Powers has often been criticised for adopting a 'conceptual approach' to its problems. But any attempt to systematise a field of activity and to recommend action must involve concepts. All that is lacking in the Committee's analysis is that the concepts are not sufficiently detailed and that nothing emerges of the difficulties which may arise from disagreement as to the meaning of lesser concepts (or words) which the Committee took for granted—such as 'dispute', 'party', 'evidence', and 'case'. Discussion of the role of ministerial decisions in planning matters, for example, has posed the question whether a 'dispute' in which a private and a public interest are opposed can properly be described as a dispute in the same sense as a conflict between private rights. Was the essential feature of the episode at Stevenage the doing of impartial justice between a proposal and objections, or the implementation of governmental and parliamentary policy?

There are a number of ways in which these alternative descriptions could be differentiated. In a critical pamphlet (*Rule of Law*) published in 1955, for example, a group of Conservative lawyers rejected the Donoughmore Committee's distinction between quasi-judicial and administrative decisions on the ground that the threat to the rights which the citizen is entitled to enjoy (itself a somewhat charged description) is essentially the same whether a dispute exists before the Minister's discretion is exercised or after. Decisions, it was suggested, should be described simply as either 'judicial' or 'discretionary'. Discretionary decisions, however, whilst not being an application of law to facts, should be required to be made on reasonable grounds whose sufficiency, it was urged, should be subject to inspection by a special Administrative Division of the High Court. This, and a number of other proposals for extending the available forms of control over administrative activity, was put before the Franks Committee in the same year.

6. *The Franks Committee Report*

The terms of reference of the Franks Committee contain no reference to quasi-judicial or administrative decisions as such. The Committee were asked to consider the working of, first, tribunals other than the ordinary courts of law, and secondly, of 'such administrative procedures as include the holding of an inquiry or hearing by or on behalf of a Minister on an appeal or as the result of objections or representations, and in particular the procedure for the compulsory purchase of land'. Although, as the Report remarks, 'the celebrated case of Crichel Down' was 'widely regarded as a principal reason for our appointment', the Committee did not consider itself authorised to consider the issues raised by that episode, or to decide whether statutory provision should be made for appeals against administrative action where no such provisions already existed. This self-denying ordinance may be regretted, since the composition of the Committee, the nature of the evidence submitted to it, and the line of inquiry which it pursued were well adapted to answering precisely that question. The larger part of the Committee's investigation could, in fact, be regarded as an attempt to discover the criteria (which the Committee on Ministers' Powers had failed to make clear) for saying that an issue should be regarded as one of 'policy', as distinct from one suitable to settlement by a tribunal or an independent arbitration.

The evidence presented on the working of existing tribunals revealed that it is far from easy to say exactly what a tribunal is, and how it differs from a body more directly concerned with the discretionary application of policy. The term '*administrative* tribunal' itself confuses this issue. The characteristic features of tribunals are those which they share with ordinary courts of law—namely independence of the executive, the application of a known and antecedent rule, a certain formality of procedure, and a final decision which is binding upon all parties and not subject to ministerial rejection or modification in the light of any considerations not present at the hearing of the issue. The characteristic features of an administrative or 'policy' decision are that it does not necessarily follow from the impartial application of a pre-existing rule, and that similar cases are not necessarily decided similarly but may be influenced by changing departmental views on other subjects. An 'administrative' tribunal if it possesses the characteristics of a tribunal deserves the adjective 'administrative' only because it is administering legislative policy in particular cases, and not because the manner of its decisions is 'administrative' in the sense used by the courts or the Committee on Ministers' Powers. It would be convenient, if it were possible, to retain the term 'tribunal' for any body of persons, whether an ordinary court of law or a special tribunal, whose decisions were impartial and independent; but it would be a delicate exercise to determine precisely which characteristics were indispensable to independence. A tribunal does not, for example, cease to be independent or judicial if its procedure is more informal than that of a court of law—unless it is very informal indeed. But what ought one to say if, for example, its members are appointed by the Government department from whose decisions they are hearing appeals; or if the tribunal gives no reasons for its decisions? In fact the bodies which are called tribunals vary considerably in their characteristics. At one end of the scale there are tribunals hearing appeals under pensions, insurance, industrial injuries, compensation, and valuation legislation which possess in practice the features characteristic of judicial bodies. The departments concerned with their operations need have no interest in the outcome of decisions beyond the interest of seeing that the relevant Acts of Parliament are properly administered, and the Minister is no more responsible to Parliament for the tribunal decisions than the Lord Chancellor is responsible for decisions reached in, for example, the county courts. Another group of tribunals may be distinguished, however, in which, though the Minister does not interfere to influence individual decisions, ministerial policy may be thought relevant to the activities of the tribunal. In some cases these bodies have been amenable to governmental influence because they are applying standards of a flexible kind. The Minister of Transport, it was said in evidence, gives directions about road transport licensing and holds conferences with the chairmen of tribunals at which licensing policy is discussed. It might be argued of such bodies that they are really only emanations of the Minister or ways of organising the department's work and not quite tribunals (though nobody, fortunately, has suggested that they should be called 'quasi-tribunals'). Certainly these bodies are approaching the borderline between independent arbitration and departmental decision. Where it is clear that a hearing with the trappings of tribunal procedure results in a decision which may be confirmed or modified by a Minister, then the borderline has been crossed. Proceedings at public local inquiries clearly fell, when the Committee came to examine them, into the last of these categories. The evidence submitted by official witnesses suggested, broadly speaking, that they should stay there. The unofficial evidence on the other hand was, with one or two exceptions, predominantly concerned to urge their removal into a more judicial sphere.

Sir Oliver Franks, in discussion with witnesses, formulated the conflict in the evidence with great clarity. There are, he said, two views of the public inquiry which precedes the ministerial confirmation of compulsory purchase or designation orders made under housing, acquisition of land, and town-planning legislation. One view is in terms of the final end of the process—the Minister's decision. Everything which takes place en route is a step by his servants to help him make the best decision. Inspectors who preside at inquiries are the Minister's eyes and ears. The other view is that of the objector who wishes to dispute what is going on. He is not content to regard the process merely as an opportunity for the administration to reflect upon its conduct but wants the decision taken to be based upon and to follow from the evidence presented by the parties at the inquiry. He wants also to know what the authority in question is proposing—what case he as an objector has to meet; and in order to meet it he wants to be able to dispute by argument and cross-examination the case of the Ministry or local authority and to see the inspector's report.

Phrases such as 'knowing the case one has to meet', or reference to 'the parties' or 'evidence', assume of course a part of what is in question, namely that the inquiry is to be viewed in a judicial light, as a confrontation of two cases. On the other hand, references to 'eyes and ears of the Minister', or to hearing objections, or to the statement that the inspector's decision should be that which the Minister would reach if he heard the case himself, beg the question in the opposite direction. On this issue the Ministry most closely concerned with public local inquiries put up a hard fight for the 'administrative' view, for departmental inspectors, and confidential reports. Dame Evelyn Sharp, Permanent Secretary to the Ministry of Housing and Local Government, argued before the Committee that the position of witnesses who had advocated an entirely independent inspectorate was incompatible with ministerial decision. It was necessary, she thought, to keep the inspectorate expert in the department's work and in touch with policy. An inquiry was only part of the process by which a Minister arrived at a decision. To publish merely a part of the scaffolding (the inspector's report) might be misleading. Identical cases might need to be decided differently. Particular disputes again might be overtaken by larger policy issues. In one case, for example, a proposal to buy a piece of land to accommodate overspill population from London had turned into a whole review of the overspill problem, and the particular proposal had been turned down, not for reasons brought out at the inquiry, but for policy reasons which were fought out afterwards in the department. The publication of reports, it was argued, would be difficult. The Minister ought not to be put in the position of being publicly in disagreement with the advice given to him by a Civil Servant. A similar situation arose over the question of cross-examination of departmental witnesses, especially if different departments were involved. Here the Treasury Solicitor felt that constitutional principles might be in danger, since to have departments controverting each other at inquiries was, he believed, contrary to the rule that the Government is one and speaks with one voice. The witnesses of the Ministry of Housing and Local Government, however, were inclined to see the difficulty of publication as being no more serious than an inconvenience which might be embarrassing to the Minister. Mr Morrison's objection to the questioning of Ministers by the Statutory Instruments Committee was phrased, it may be recalled, in a similar fashion. Perhaps a foreign reader of British Blue Books might be forgiven for imagining that the primary principle of the Constitution is the preservation of Ministers from embarrassment.

A number of witnesses were pressed to say whether they could formulate tests for distinguishing issues which raised matters of 'policy' from issues which did not. The 'advice' given by an inspector is clearly made up of elements which do not all resemble the policy advice given by higher Civil Servants in the course of administration, and publication of the factual elements of his recommendation, or even the recommendation itself in cases where one was made, would not, it was contended, raise constitutional issues at all. It was also open to doubt whether advice on matters of fact sought afterwards by a Minister within his own or another department was necessarily information which must be preserved under the umbrella of ministerial secrecy. What could be considered as 'factual' was of course open to dispute. Lord Justice Parker at several points suggested to witnesses that questions which they were treating as questions of policy were of a type which courts decide every day as questions of fact. A number of the unofficial legal witnesses who submitted evidence shared an implicit major premiss that the policy of Ministers should wherever possible be made as much like a system of case law as possible. Planning policy, it was suggested, for example, should grow more and more explicit and be formulated in a series of more and more concrete generalisations. The Inns of Court Conservative and Unionist Association took a somewhat unexpected line, however, on the 'concretisation' of policy. Under examination by the Committee they were prepared to say that 'policy' must begin and end where the

Minister said it did, and that a Minister might wish to apply 'policy' to an individual case—though, they added, it was important to get Ministers to draw the line clearly between policy and non-policy matters, wherever they wished to place it. There is an important truth about the meaning of 'policy' contained in this admission. The word is one which implies generality and issues of principle. 'Properly understood,' it has been argued, 'policy should be limited to the ultimate value judgments'[1] involved in administration. But, as Mrs Ruth Glass and Professor Griffith suggested, decisions of a less elevated kind and the criteria by which they are reached may be concealed behind the 'magic spell' of policy which could function as 'an umbrella term for value judgments and technical criteria' and as 'a pretext for failure to define either'.[2] A boundary line, they said in evidence, could be drawn at the point where decisions could be arrived at by an expert or a tribunal according to verifiable technical criteria. Wherever this was possible in the planning field, disputes about the policy applied to the regulation and control of land might be resolved by a tribunal. The policy itself might thereby become articulate, consistent, and 'hived off' from ministerial discretion. One difficulty about 'policy', however, is the relation between it and politics. In principle a policy matter may be expected to be of political significance because being of general application and affecting a number of people is one way of being important and politically charged. But any issue may become politically charged, and it may or may not be a type of question for which it is possible in principle to lay down reasonably objective criteria. In other words, the technical possibilities of cutting down the scope of ministerial policy and discretionary decisions may cut across the political or emotional possibilities. The latter may depend at any one time more upon the existing feelings and prejudices of Ministers and Members as to the issues which can be 'taken out of politics' than upon the logical feasibility of a judicial form of arbitration.

The Committee's Report which appeared in July 1957 contained, in the event, noticeably less philosophising than its predecessor of 1932. Beyond saying that administrative procedures should be characterised by 'openness, fairness, and impartiality' and that 'the individual has the right to enjoy his property without interference from the administration unless the interference is unmistakably justified in the public interest' (discoveries which would hardly in themselves have justified an expenditure of £21,216), the Report contained

1. J. A. G. Griffith and H. Street, *Principles of Administrative Law* (2nd ed.), p. 150.

2. Evidence of Mrs Ruth Glass and Professor Griffith. Day 21, p. 982.

few theoretical propositions. Nevertheless to shun philosophical commitment is itself a philosophy, and the Committee's Anglican conclusions that a reasonable balance should be struck between the conflicting interests, and that neither the judicial nor the administrative views of public inquiry procedure should be emphasised at the expense of the other, were not commonplaces. They were, in fact, a doctrine with a slightly radical air, if only because the 'administrative' view which pervades British institutions rarely had seriously been balanced against any other view in a neutral non-party setting. Under both parts of its terms of reference, in fact, the Committee aimed a number of blows at the 'public interest principle'. One of its most general and striking conclusions was that when decisions are taken on methods of adjudicating disputes between individuals and the administration, preference should be given, if not to the courts, to an administrative tribunal rather than to a Minister, and that every opportunity should be taken of expressing policy in the form of regulations capable of being administered in a judicial way. Existing tribunals, the Committee thought, 'should properly be regarded as machinery provided by Parliament for adjudication rather than as part of the machinery of administration'. For 'Although the relevant statutes do not in all cases expressly enact that tribunals are to consist entirely of persons outside the Government service, the use of the term "tribunal" in legislation undoubtedly bears this connotation, and the intention of Parliament to provide for the independence of tribunals is clear and unmistakable.' Moreover, the Committee concluded, a general appeal on points of law should be possible from all tribunals; legal representation should be possible in all cases; hearings should be public; reasons should always be given; chairmen of tribunals should be appointed by the Lord Chancellor, and independent councils should be set up to supervise their operations.

It is noteworthy that the Committee used the terms 'adjudication' and 'adjudicative' both in speaking of tribunals and in their later discussion of public inquiries. In the first case the word seems to be merely a synonym for 'judicial', but in the latter case it is specifically denied that an inquiry is a judicial process or that the principle of impartiality can be applied to it without qualification. Here 'adjudicative' was the Committee's own contribution to the vocabulary of politics, derived from its balancing of the two views of the inquiry procedure. A Minister, the Report conceded, could not be restricted, as a judge would be, to a decision reached only on the material brought before an inquiry; nor could he be prevented from changing his policy or consulting other departments after the evidence had been heard; but additional factual evidence obtained in such a way ought to be placed before objectors.[1] A procedure subject to restrictions of this kind and accompanied by increased rights of cross-examination of departmental witnesses is a noticeable inroad into the administrative view, though it leaves ministerial responsibility untouched. The process of deciding under these conditions is one for which a new descriptive term is badly needed.

7. *The Tribunals and Inquiries Act, 1958*

The Government's reaction to the Franks Committee's proposals was flatteringly rapid. The Report was debated in October 1957 and the Home Secretary announced that 71 of the 95 recommendations were to be accepted without substantial reservations. Others were accepted in modified form. The supervision of tribunals was to be undertaken by a single Council set up jointly by the Lord Chancellor and the Secretary of State for Scotland. Less eagerness was shown in pursuing the appearance of impartiality which the Committee had sought in its recommendations that tribunal members and inspectors presiding over public inquiries should be independent appointments. Ministers, in the Government's view, must continue to be entrusted with these appointments but consultation with the Council on tribunals and the Lord Chancellor (for inspectors) would precede them. In the Commons' debate on the Report the proposals were welcomed with equal enthusiasm on both sides of the House. Only one member (Mr R. T. Paget) could be found to support the tarnished administrative doctrine against the Committee's modest revision. The tendency of a multiplication of legal formalities, he argued, would be to protect Ministers from parliamentary criticism and to impede the machinery for the public acquisition of land. The terms 'fairness' and 'impartiality' could not properly be applied to public inquiries at all and were 'just wind'. (Sir Hartley Shawcross when Attorney-General had perhaps the more delicate metaphor in his reference to the inquiry procedure as an opportunity 'to let off steam'.)

Whilst a number of the Franks recommendations were put into effect by administrative action, and by statutory instruments prescribing codes of procedure later drafted by the Ministry of Housing and Local Government and the Scottish Departments concerned with public inquiries, the proposals that required legislation were

1. This caused trouble. See *Council on Tribunals Report* (1961) and Griffith, 'The Council and the Chalk Pit', *Public Administration* (1961, vol. 31), p. 369. It was eventually provided for by regulation. See Town and Country Planning (Inquiries Procedure) Rules, 1969.

embodied in the Tribunals and Inquiries Act of 1958. A 'tribunal' is not defined by the Act. Instead, more than thirty bodies are listed by name—beginning with the Agricultural Lands Tribunals and concluding with the Commissioners of Inland Revenue—as falling under the supervision of the Council and its Scottish Committee. The Council itself consists of not more than fifteen or less than ten members[1] and its duties are defined as the keeping under review of the constitution and working of tribunals and the reporting from time to time on such matters as it may deem to be of special importance (or which may be referred to it) with respect to administrative procedures involving a statutory inquiry. An annual report of the proceedings of the Council and its Scottish Committee is made to the Lord Chancellor and to the Secretary of State, who must lay the annual reports before Parliament with such comments as they think fit. The Government did not appear, however, entirely to have accepted the logic of the Franks Committee's conclusion that the tribunal structure with its adjudicatory purpose ought not to be treated as a part of the machinery of administration. One ground for the decision not to allow the members of tribunals to be appointed by the Council rather than by departments was stated by the Attorney-General and the Lord Chancellor to be the preservation of parliamentary accountability. The Lord Chancellor is of course responsible for appointing the members of the Council on Tribunals and it is not clear what sort of accountability not covered by this would be proper in respect of a process whose functioning is acknowledged to lie outside the sphere of responsibility of departmental Ministers.

The Act in part implemented the proposal for appeal on a point of law from the majority of tribunals, with special exceptions such as the National Insurance and Industrial Injuries Commissioners and the National Assistance Appeal Tribunal. It also provided that effect should no longer be given to words in earlier statutes precluding review by prerogative orders of tribunal decisions. The increased scope for recourse to the latter remedies, though merely making explicit a position which the courts seemed to have reached quite apart from the Act,[2] raises a potential problem of some importance about the purposes which the legislature intended tribunals to fulfil.

1. The trade unions, agriculture and land-owning, public administration, the social services, industry, and the legal profession are represented on the Council. The first Report which appeared in 1960 stated that about 2,000 tribunals fall under the Council's supervision. For an account of the Council's work, see H. W. R. Wade: 'The Council on Tribunals', *Public Law* (1960), p. 351; and J. F. Garner, 'The Council on Tribunals', *Public Law* (1965), p. 321.

2. cf. *R. v. Medical Appeal Tribunal, ex parte Gilmore* [1957] 2 WLR 498.

As both the Committee on Ministers' Powers and the Franks Committee noted, the function of tribunals in administering welfare legislation was to fulfil the need for disputes, usually of a fairly minor kind, to be settled speedily, cheaply, and informally, by specialised adjudicators familiar with the technical problems of, for example, medicine, valuation, engineering, or industrial injuries. It may be that it was wrong and mistaken of the legislature to provide that many of these decisions should be 'final' or 'conclusive for all purposes' or that they should not 'be called in question in any court of law'. But few laymen reading these words would feel any doubt that Parliament had intended to stop up recourse to the ordinary courts from the decisions of tribunals and to give them an absolute discretion in the performance of their adjudicative function. In dealing with tribunals (as distinct from Ministers) the courts, however, have come very near on occasion to implying that they will not treat Parliament's words, however plain, as conveying an intention altogether to oust the jurisdiction of the courts. 'It is axiomatic,' said Lord Justice Denning (as he then was) in *Barnard v. National Dock Labour Board*, 'that when a statutory tribunal sits to administer justice it must act in accordance with the law. Parliament clearly so intended.'[1] It might have seemed arguable to a layman (and particularly to anyone who suspected the judiciary of a lack of sympathy with the objects of social service legislation) that though Parliament naturally intended all tribunals to make their decisions correctly and in accordance with the law, the only point in using such emphatic language was to condone misinterpretations of law and fact by tribunals operating within their jurisdiction, for the sake of the benefits of rapid and informal decision. Whatever Parliament may have intended, it has, in passing the Tribunals and Inquiries Act, decided against this view and now openly commanded what was previously imputed to it, sometimes unplausibly. A question of law decided 'finally' and 'conclusively' by a tribunal may be reviewed by *certiorari*, even in the case of those expert tribunals exempted from the provision for a straight appeal. The courts are hardly likely to interfere with these tribunal determinations on a wide scale, but the open recognition of the possibility together with the more extensive scope for appeal on points of law marks a significant change in attitude towards judicial controls. This change in the climate of feeling probably owes something to the Franks Committee and has become even more noticeable since the passing of the 1958 Act.

Where Ministers themselves and their departments are involved

1. [1953] 2 QB 18 at 41. cf. the *Anisminic* case [1969] 2 AC 147.

the administrative reforms instituted by the Government and the Act of 1958 both left untouched the question of principle which the Franks Committee declined to answer: To what extent, if any, can discretionary decisions by Government departments be subjected to restraints or control additional to that obtainable in the political atmosphere of the Commons as an incidental by-product of the struggle between Government and Opposition? In the main there seemed to be three possible answers. The first was simply 'Not at all'. This might be called the Democratic Administrators' doctrine. The administration, on this view, represents the public interest. The government can be changed and individuals who find themselves adversely affected by an administrative process authorised by Parliament cannot reasonably expect any form of arbitration or appeal beyond the existing opportunities for political agitation by which the rights of Englishmen have traditionally been protected.

A second answer, which might for want of any better term be called the Legalist doctrine, saw the problem as one of setting up an appropriate institution to impose upon administrative decisions controls of a kind analogous to those imposed in Europe by administrative courts. Suggestions were presented to the Franks Committee for two such institutions—an Administrative Division of the High Court or alternatively a General Administrative Appeal Tribunal. The Committee did not feel able to comment however on the proposal made by the sponsors of each body that it should have as one of its functions the hearing of appeals against allegations of harsh or unfair administrative decisions.

The third answer could be termed the Additional Publicity doctrine. Like the Legalist view it could cite working analogies and institutions from abroad. In several Scandinavian countries, it was pointed out, an independent Commissioner, appointed by Parliament, was given the task of investigating complaints about the working of all state administrative organs.[1] In 1961, *Justice* (the British Section of the International Commission of Jurists) published a set of proposals for a British Parliamentary Commissioner or 'Ombudsman'.[2]

1. There is now a large body of literature on the operation of Parliamentary Commissioners in various countries. See the essays and bibliography in D. E. Rowat, *The Ombudsman* (2nd ed. 1968), and W. Gellhorn, *Citizens Protectors in Nine Countries* (1967).

2. See *The Citizen and the Administration: the Redress of Grievances* (The Whyatt Report), (1961).

8. *The Parliamentary Commissioner*

These suggestions did not find favour with Mr Macmillan's Government, which dismissed them in a ministerial statement of under a dozen lines as being incompatible with the principle of ministerial responsibility to Parliament.

The return of a Labour Government in 1964 (with ombudsman proposals in its electoral manifesto) led however to renewed interest in the *Justice* proposals and a White Paper and draft Bill were produced which followed the main outlines of the New Zealand Parliamentary Commissioner (Ombudsman) Act of 1962. The Bill laid before Parliament in October 1965 proposed that the Parliamentary Commissioner should be confined in his inquiries to central departments (excluding local government, nationalised industries and police) and that access should be by written complaint transmitted by a Member of Parliament. No ministerial veto on inquiries was proposed, but publication of information in the Commissioner's reports (even presumably to a Select Committee) might be prevented by a ministerial objection taken on grounds of security or public interest.

The Act embodying these proposals came into effect on 1 April 1967. A crucial question about the Parliamentary Commissioner's function is raised by S. 12 (3) of the Act, which forbids the Commissioner to question the merits of a decision taken without maladministration by a government department or other authority in the exercise of a discretion vested in that department or authority. The implied attempt to distinguish between the merits or substance of a decision and the procedure by which a decision is reached highlights an uncertainty inherent from the beginning in the debate on the redress of grievances by ombudsmen. Talk of citizens' grievances, or the redress of bureaucratic injustice, leaves a number of questions unclear. One is whether grievances or injustices that stem from legislation (or departmental sub-legislation) should be amenable to scrutiny. Another is whether the system should act merely as a control of procedural errors and abuses or also as an avenue for securing or recommending the reversal of allegedly wrong or unwelcome discretionary decisions at whatever level in the departmental hierarchy they are taken and even if they do not embody abuses or improper use of the decision procedures. Supported by the Parliamentary Select Committee set up by the House of Commons the Parliamentary Commissioner has, despite the discouraging form of the 1967 Act, extended his inquiries to include departmental rules and what has been described by him as the potentially 'bad decision'—one that is so defective on its face as to imply that the processes by which it was reached must necessarily have been defective. Since neither the draftsman of the Act nor anyone else has ever been able to define what makes a bad decision bad, it is in these areas that the most interesting future exercises of ombudsmanship will obviously lie.[1]

1. The Commissioner's annual reports for the years 1967–70 show the following results:

	Cases Received	*Rejected (outside jurisdiction)*	*Maladministration Found*
1967	1,069	561	19
1968	1,120	727	38
1969	761	445	48
1970	645	362	59

cf. below pp. 149–50 on Ministers, Civil Servants and the Parliamentary Commissioner. On the working of the 1967 Act see G. Marshall, 'Parliament and the Ombudsman' (in *Parliament in Transition* Ed. A. H. Hanson and B. Crick); Paul Jackson, 'The Work of the Parliamentary Commissioner for Administration' [1971] *Publication* 39; and David Foulkes, 'The Discretionary Provisions of the Parliamentary Commissioner Act, 1967' 34 Mod. Law Rev. 377 (1971).

7

PARLIAMENTARY PRIVILEGE

1. *Public pressure and influence*

A number of constitutional questions about the relations between Ministers, Members, and the public in general has emerged from some recent episodes revolving around the modern application of the law and custom of Parliament. Few better examples could be found, not merely of the difference between the theory of the Constitution and its changing practical conventions, but also of the potential conflict between theories not quite rejected and practices not quite received. In twentieth-century practice Members of Parliament find themselves in a House of Commons which is not at all the assemblage of free-thinking senatorial minds controlling the administration on behalf of the people which was portrayed so sternly by Edmund Burke to his Bristol electors. The organisation of political parties within Parliament and outside; the quasi-respectability of the doctrine of the mandate as applied to governments collectively; and the growth of sectional interest and pressure groups seeking to influence legislation and legislators in particular directions have between them fashioned parliamentary freedom of conscience and action in a totally different image. Yet we continue to believe that Members ought not to be thought of as the delegates of their electors. Moreover, the law and custom of Parliament which deal with its privileges as a legislative body really rest upon the older theory, and parts of that theory continue on occasion to be asserted. The tension between the rights of Members as 'attorneys for the people of England' and the rights of the electorate to express and impress its wishes upon the legislature is not indeed entirely a product of changing political conditions. It is one which has always been inherent in English law—in the notorious dualism between the authority of each House of Parliament to define and assert its own privileges on the one hand, and the rights of the electorate defined by the ordinary courts of law on the other. Perhaps the twentieth century has neither found nor needed a Wilkes or a Bradlaugh to challenge the legislature on behalf of the rights of electors, but parliamentarians have been unable entirely to ignore the signs of a different and milder clash of jurisdictions inherent in the fact that Parliament is no longer the exclusive stage upon which public policy is debated; and its undoubted legal supremacy, dignity, and pre-eminence must be interpreted in an electoral environment radically transformed by organisation, political and otherwise, by radio, press, public opinion polling, and television debating. In this sphere minor conventions emerge and feelings about them change with remarkable speed. An example might be seen in the agreed abrogation of the rule formerly restraining the broadcast discussion, within a period of fourteen days, of topics about to be debated in the House. In 1955, when asked to consider a modification of the embargo, Sir Winston Churchill replied: 'I will never reconsider it. I believe it would be a shocking thing to have debates in this House forestalled time after time by the expression of opinion of persons who have not the status and responsibilities of Members. . . . I am quite sure that the bringing on of exciting debates in these vast new robot organisations of television and BBC broadcasting timed to take place before a debate in this House may have very deleterious effects upon our general interest.'[1] This attitude seems, as it seemed to many at its inception, impossibly restrictive of the public's right to hear and engage in free discussion of current political issues, and the suggestions implied in the phrase 'forestalling of debate' exaggerated; but the problem may still be posed. How, today, ought the principle to be applied that Members have the right freely to debate without undesirable influence, pressure, or interference from outside? Of what does undesirable interference consist?

A survey of the proceedings of the House of Commons' Committee of Privileges during the past thirty years indicates clearly that there is great difficulty in defining simply what is and what is not an improper interference with the rights of Members. The difficulty lies in applying principles and precedents, which were developed in the struggle to secure popular and parliamentary liberties from interference by the Crown, to the situation produced by the emergence of organised pressure from the electorate.

The freedom of Members to speak and vote without restraint is one of the well-recognised privileges of Parliament. It was expressed in the terms of a fifteenth-century petition, cited to the Committee of Privileges in 1947, as 'the old liberte and fredom of the Comyns of this lande . . . to speke and say in the House of their assemble, as to

1. 537 HC Deb., 5s., c. 1277.

theym is thought convenient or reasonable without any maner chalenge, charge or punycion'. The Bill of Rights provides that debates in Parliament are not to be 'impeached or questioned' in any court or place outside of Parliament. The basis of the privilege is the protection of Members from molestation in the discharge of their duty to speak and vote. Except in this, their parliamentary capacity, Members do not enjoy the protection of privilege. In 1887, for example, the Speaker refused to rule that a *prima facie* breach of privilege had been committed by an article in *The Times* which stated that certain Members 'draw at once their living and their notoriety from the steady perpetration of crimes for which civilisation demands the gallows'.[1] In more recent times, however, milder forms of expression than this have been thought to reflect upon the professional dignity of Members.

The boundary lines between free comment, legitimate pressure, and improper interference are obviously not easy to formulate in principle. It is not in principle improper or a breach of privilege to lobby one's Member or to take part in a collective lobby or campaign to exert pressure on a Member of Parliament or a number of Members of Parliament. It was, however, suggested in 1953 that a breach of privilege had been committed by the members of an association who, in a circular to Members of Parliament, stated that they would use their trade contacts with constituents to bring pressure to bear against a particular legislative measure. The Committee of Privileges advised that the circular, though undesirable, was not improper. Campaigns by organised interests to organise opposition to legislative proposals (nationalisation or denationalisation measures, for example) appear to come into a similar category. Certain forms of pressure on Members of Parliament are now presumably not to be accounted impediments to freewill on the score that they are a part of the national environment. Amongst these must be placed the activities of the Party Whips. There seem to have been few attempts to challenge the constitutional propriety of pressure from this quarter. In December 1956, however, a brave attempt was made to persuade the Speaker that a *Daily Herald* article which referred to 'unexampled pressures . . . used to force Tories into line' might contain material to support the view that privilege had been breached by somebody. But Mr Speaker considered that the activities of Whips and the usual channels had never hitherto been regarded as a breach of the privileges of the whole House.[2]

The growth of informal and sometimes formal arrangements be-

1. 311 Parl. Db. (1887), c. 286. cf. HC 149 (1950–1) (Clan-Briton case).
2. 578 HC Deb., c. 408.

tween professional and trade associations, trade unions and interest groups outside the House, and Members who undertake to put the point of view of such groups when legislation affecting them comes before the House, raises delicate questions on both sides of the relationship. Mr W. J. Brown, who in 1947 was acting as 'Parliamentary General Secretary' for the Civil Service Clerical Association, claimed that an attempt by the Association to terminate the arrangement after disagreement over his political views was an improper threat to penalise him in respect of his conduct in Parliament. In 1944 a similar claim was made by Mr W. A. Robinson, Labour Member of Parliament for Saint Helens, when the trade union which had sponsored his parliamentary candidature called upon him to resign. In each case the Committee of Privileges refused to say that any breach of privilege had been committed. It was conceded that 'punitive or discriminatory action' by outside bodies could not be extended to include the reproof or censure of a political representative, though it might possibly include a threat to withdraw financial support as a specific threat to influence parliamentary action on a particular issue. Merely to seek to terminate an agreement can of course only be construed as a form of pressure because the agreement exists, and it might seem that Members of Parliament themselves are acting improperly in placing themselves in any relationship which can be construed as imposing a contractual obligation to pursue any particular course of action. In Mr Brown's case his agreement specified that he should be entitled to engage in his political activities with complete freedom, and the House of Commons subsequently agreed to a resolution stating that any contractual arrangement, whether involving financial reward or not, which fettered a Member's complete independence would be improper. The duty of a Member, the resolution concluded, was to his constituents and to the country as a whole, rather than to any particular section thereof.[1]

The principles laid down by Burke, and, it would seem, implicitly endorsed by the House, do not appear to extend so as to prevent the use of political sanctions by constituency associations to penalise past actions of a Member or to secure compliance with particular views. A local political club, in March 1958, could threaten a Labour Member that electoral opposition would be organised unless a Private Member's Bill then before the House were withdrawn. Again, in the previous year, the constituency Conservative Association in Bournemouth East and Christchurch was able to expel its Member, Mr Nigel Nicolson, from the Association and inform him that he was not to be readopted in view of his opposition to the Government's Suez inter-

1. 440 HC Deb., cs. 284–5.

vention; and it was not felt (at least by Bournemouth Conservatives) that the action was a constitutionally improper interference with the Member's freedom of judgment.

If political threats and sanctions against individual Members are legitimate, however, it is not easy to see why it should have been held a breach of privilege in 1946 for a number of constituents to put up in London and Westminster, before a debate in the Commons, posters threatening to publish the names of all Members of Parliament voting for bread rationing as 'public enemies and dictators'. It must be concluded that, whether the offence be described as an insult, as intimidation, or as obstruction, at least certain forms of political action, in addition to financial threats or inducements, may infringe the House's privileges. The same is true of communications to Members. The editor of the *Sunday Graphic*, in December 1956, urged those of his readers who dissented from the views of an Opposition Member to telephone their opinions directly to him, and supplied the requisite number. After a large number of calls had been made the Member in question was compelled to disconnect his telephone and the editor was summoned before the Committee of Privileges. He submitted that it was not uncommon for the electorate to be exhorted to write or telegraph their opinions to Members and that the telephone was a simpler and more direct way of achieving the same object. The Committee advised, however, that a serious breach of privilege had been committed. No similar case of molestation had occurred in the past, but the application of the principle that a Member must not be molested on account of his conduct in Parliament was clear. 'Whether communications to Members of Parliament by constituents or others amount to an improper interference . . .', the Committee reported, 'depends on the nature and manner of the communications.'[1]

That Members have a right to communicate freely with constituents may itself raise further queries, both in respect of physical and written communication. The action of the police in preventing access of constitutents to St Stephen's Hall, in the course of dispersing a disorderly crowd, has been raised as a matter of privilege. It does not seem, however, that the right of a Member of Parliament to perform his duties without impediment can be interpreted so as to prevent interference with those who wish to communicate with him physically[2] or by letter. In March 1955 Mr Tom Driberg complained that pressure had been brought to bear upon an army constituent to withdraw allegations which had led to the asking of a parliamentary

1. HC 27 (1956–7). cf. Mr Jordan's case, HC 284 (1959–60).
2. Some constituents, for example, are in prison. cf. HC 189 (1970–1).

question, but the Committee of Privileges reported that it could find no precedent for treating an attempt to influence the nature or content of a communication to a Member as a breach of privilege.[1] In the Commons it was argued that the offence was that of attempting 'to prevent subsequent proceedings which might have taken place in this House'.[2] The category of events outside the House which might be alleged to satisfy this description is clearly dangerously wide.

2. *Public criticism*

Speeches and writings reflecting on either House or its Members need separate consideration. May calls them 'constructive contempts'.[3] In theory any writing or report which describes proceedings in the House is a breach of privilege (though one which the Houses have long condoned), since the orders passed in the seventeenth and eighteenth centuries prohibiting publication of debates may still be enforced. An article in the *Sunday Express* in 1953, which in purporting to describe events during an all-night sitting of the House referred to two women Members as sleeping in a retiring room (some editions contained the word 'snoring'), was treated as a contempt of a kind tending to lower the House in public esteem. The older prohibitions aiming to suppress the reporting of speeches presumably rested on different grounds.

Unfavourable comment about the conduct of Members plainly merges by degrees into criticism of the House, and this is not always easily distinguishable from criticism (perhaps distorted or exaggerated) of party attitudes or of legislative or administrative measures. Nor is every breach, as the Committee remarked in 1953, worthy of occupying the attention of the House (though the House's standards seem to vary from time to time). The impropriety in question was a headline in the *Daily Worker* to an article on the Housing Repairs and Rents Bill, which ran, 'Members of Parliament Vote Money Into Their Own Pockets'. Some complaints, indeed, have rested upon reasoning which might without understatement be called 'constructive' in the worst sense of that term. In 1952 complaint was raised of a newspaper letter which implicitly reflected (it was urged) upon the conduct of the Chair by arguing that obstruction had been permitted to take place in Committee. On 6 December 1955 Mr Silverman drew the attention of the House to a report in the *Belfast Telegraph* of a speech by the chairman of the North Tyrone Unionist Association, in which Mr Charles Beattie, who had been disqualified from Mem-

1. HC 112 (1954–5).
2. 538 HC Deb., 5s., cs. 1607–16.
3. *Parliamentary Practice* (18th ed.), p. 140.

bership of the House, was said to have been 'pilloried over a legal quibble'. The only way, Mr Silverman suggested, in which this could have happened was as the result of the suggestion of the Leader of the House that the matter should be referred to a Select Committee. This (he argued) was a criticism of Parliament and its officers.

The difficulty of distinguishing permissible, if unfair, political comment from illegitimate reflection was presented in its most acute form in recent years during the Suez crisis of 1956. Commenting upon the imposition of petrol rationing, the *Sunday Express* printed an article under the heading 'Privilege' which contained (amidst some elaboration) the statements that 'Tomorrow a time of hardship starts for everyone. For everyone? Include the politicians out of that. Petrol rationing will pass them by. They are to get prodigious supplementary allowances. . . . What are Members of Parliament doing about this monstrous injustice. . . . There is not a squeak of protest.' On the following day the article was referred to the Committee of Privileges, and on subsequent days further complaints were raised in the House about similar implications in a political cartoon, in the BBC programme *Any Questions* and in a provincial newspaper, the *Romford Recorder*. Though the cartoonist, the provincial editor, and the broadcaster were spared, the Committee of Privileges concluded that the editor of the *Sunday Express* had been guilty of a serious contempt in reflecting upon all Members of the House and so upon the House itself. The word 'politicians' in the article would ordinarily be understood to mean Members of Parliament, the Report continued, and the editor had '*inter alia* intended to hold them up to public obloquy as the result of their alleged failure to protest against unfair discrimination of which they were the beneficiaries'.[1] He should be severely reprimanded. Accordingly, the editor appeared at the Bar of the House and made his humble apology.

The House's action in the case of the *Sunday Express* poses in the clearest way the question whether the undoubted legal privileges of Parliament ought to be exercised at the present time to protect Members against the pressures of public criticism, however unfair. Since an intention to bring into hatred or contempt Her Majesty, the Government and Constitution, or either House of Parliament appears to be seditious at common law, it would seem to be possible to prosecute any gross offence as a seditious libel in the ordinary courts. If any libel cannot be shown to amount to a contempt for this purpose, it is questionable whether it ought to be punished at all. Objection

1. HC 38 (1956–7), p. 5.

might be raised to the present procedure on the ground that no disputed question of fact or law can properly be decided under conditions in which the protections normally thought necessary for accused persons in the courts (public hearing, legal representation, and a right to cross-examine) do not apply. The unfailingly obsequious attitude of twentieth-century offenders charged with breaches of privilege is, perhaps, in part a consequence of the procedural conditions and of the fact that the insufficiently apologetic demeanour of alleged offenders is a consideration which often appears to rank high in the House's consideration of the sanction to be imposed. (No action was taken in 1956 for example against the editor of the *Sunday Graphic* on the ground that—as the Committee said—he 'had not sought to justify his conduct'.) The mode of punishment involved was the cause of some disquiet in Australia in 1955 when the proprietor of a New South Wales newspaper and a journalist employed by him were committed to prison by the House of Representatives after being charged with a breach of its privileges (which the High Court of Australia and, on appeal, the Privy Council, held to be those of the House of Commons). Mr Menzies later declared himself ready to give consideration to a review of the machinery for declaring and enforcing parliamentary privilege. One precedent for procedural reform in this country could be found in the decision of 1868 to relinquish the House's jurisdiction over disputed elections and transfer it to the courts—a recognition of the fact that the House is not well adapted to the performance of judicial functions.

The House of Commons itself appears to be divided in its views on these matters. When, in 1957, six Government backbenchers tabled a motion proposing that a report be drawn up defining and clarifying the present purpose of parliamentary privilege, Mr R. A. Butler, the Leader of the House, found himself unable to support it. He believed, with Blackstone, that 'the dignity and independence of the two Houses are in great measure preserved by keeping their privileges indefinite'. Blackstone's reason, however, was the tactical one that a precise predetermination by the Commons of the limits of their privileges might enable the Crown to erode the Commons' liberties in ways which fell outside the lines drawn; and it is difficult to agree that this consideration should today take precedence over the general principle, inherent in the rule of law, that offences should be known and defined beforehand with as much precision as possible. A conceivable objection to a statute transferring jurisdiction to the High Court might be that an impossibly lengthy enumeration of contempts and breaches of privilege might have to be made. But it could be argued that a statutory formula based upon May's definition of a contempt would suffice both for this and for the wider concept of breach of privilege. There might be disagreement about the relative virtues of judicial and parliamentary decision in this field.[1] It would probably not be disputed, however, that the basis of both the specific privilege of freedom of speech and the right to punish for contempt is the free working of legislative institutions. A contempt, as defined by Erskine May, is an act whose direct or indirect result is to obstruct or impede either House in the performance of its functions. Whether alleged contempt or breach of privilege had substantially this result would be an issue upon which the courts could pronounce in at least as objective a way as they are already called to do in other fields where general statutory definitions have to be applied. There is some evidence that whilst objective views of this question are taken by the House in normal times, they cannot equally be relied upon at times of political excitement. The power directly to punish contempts not committed in its presence is, it may be noted, not one which has an obvious connection with the work of a legislative body at all. No such power originally inhered in other British legislatures in the colonial empire, since it derives in law not from the legislative but from the now anachronistic judicial powers of the High Court of Parliament. No analogous power is exercised by either House of Congress in the United States.

3. *The freedom of debate and 'proceedings'*

The immunity of Members from external pressures and interference, and the freedom which is guaranteed by the Bill of Rights from question or 'impeachment' by outsiders, includes absolute immunity at law for words spoken in the chamber of the House. The duties of Members include under modern conditions, however, many things besides speaking in debate. The control of the House over Ministers involves the putting down of parliamentary questions about the work of the departments and about matters arising outside the House. As the result of the expansion of governmental control in the economic field Ministers have acquired certain responsibilities for the operations of the nationalised industries, and the supervisory functions of the House may be performed in part (and especially where Ministers do not answer questions about the day-to-day operation of public corporations) by writing directly to the chairmen of boards, or to other persons outside the House. Does the absolute immunity of parliamentary 'proceedings' protect a Member in pursuing these

1. cf. *The Times* correspondence: 27 March, 6, 10, 24 April 1947, on the case of Mr Junor.

extended activities which are now thought to be part of the Member's functions but which obviously did not exist when the Bill of Rights was framed? It is curious that this question should never have been seriously posed until 1957, when Mr G. R. Strauss raised as a question of privilege a communication from solicitors representing the London Electricity Board. Mr Strauss had criticised the policy of the Board in fairly strong terms in a letter to the Paymaster General. Since the matter (the method of disposal of used cables) was one of day-to-day administration, the Minister had forwarded the letter to the Board, which, after some discussion with Mr Strauss, informed him that it intended to institute libel proceedings against him. The Committee of Privileges reported to the House that the Member's letter could properly be described as a 'proceeding in Parliament' and that the London Electricity Board had been guilty of a breach of privilege. The question was complicated, however, by the fact that the Committee could not decide whether the Parliamentary Privilege Act of 1770 affected the issue, and therefore recommended that the House seek an opinion from the Judicial Committee of the Privy Council. When the Report was debated in the House[1] it was urged with some feeling that the reference of a matter affecting the House's privileges to an outside body was detrimental to its dignity. 'This question of Privilege,' said Mr Ede, 'if taken outside the House, means the end of parliamentary democracy as we know it.' He viewed the attempt to arrive at a precise and exact definition of privilege 'with great terror'. Other Members none the less seemed prepared to contemplate more precise definitions of the limits of parliamentary immunity. Sir Lionel Heald criticised the Committee's argument that since Members, dissatisfied with replies to letters, might seek satisfaction in the House, their correspondence with Ministers could be regarded as a 'proceeding in Parliament'. He did not think it a good reason for regarding something as a 'proceeding' that it might become a 'proceeding'. Mr Herbert Morrison, too, thought that the immunity conceded to freedom of speech in the chamber of the House, where reply could be made, ought not to extend to correspondence with a Minister. Letters might, for example, be written or forwarded containing malicious imputations about the character or professional abilities of employees of the nationalised industries or other private persons. To extend absolute privilege to them was, he thought, from the citizen's point of view, 'a bit hot'.

On a division a majority of the House were in favour of taking the opinion of the Judicial Committee on the Act of 1770. That Act and

1. 578 HC Deb., 5s. c. 397 ff. (4 December 1957).

three earlier statutes provided, in apparently explicit terms, that actions brought against Members of either House should not be 'impeached, stayed or delayed by or under colour or pretence of any privilege of Parliament'.

In May 1958 the Judicial Committee delivered its advice. The Acts in question (their Lordships decided), although they appeared explicit, must be taken to refer only to actions against Members as private persons (e.g. for debts and conduct as individuals) and not to suits in respect of a Member's conduct in Parliament. If the words of the Act applied so as to authorise judgment to be given in a proceeding involving speech or conduct in Parliament the effect would have been substantially to repeal the ninth section of the Bill of Rights which protected the freedom of speech in Parliament. The conclusion that this privilege solemnly asserted in the Bill of Rights was within a few years abrogated could not lightly be reached. Their Lordships had been reminded of the way in which from the earliest times the right of free speech had been asserted. Strode's Act, passed in the fourth year of Henry VIII, had declared that all suits and proceedings against Richard Strode and any other Member of Parliament 'for any bill, speaking or declaring of any matter concerning the Parliament to be communed and treated of, be utterly void and of non effect'. The question referred to their Lordships must then be answered by saying that the House would not be acting contrary to the Acts of 1700 and 1770 if it treated the issue of a writ against a Member of Parliament in respect of a speech or proceeding by him in Parliament as a breach of its privileges.[1]

The Judicial Committee's advice, it must be noticed, related only to the interpretation of the Parliamentary Privilege Act. It remains true that, whilst the Commons would not be acting contrary to that Act in treating the issue of a writ against a Member as a breach of privilege, they might nevertheless be acting contrary to common law. The Judicial Committee dropped a strong hint on this point at the close of their report. In refraining from expressing any opinion upon the question whether at common law the mere issue of a writ could in any circumstances be a breach of privilege, they were 'mindful of the inalienable right of Her Majesty's subjects to have recourse to her courts of law for the remedy of their wrongs'.

In recommending that the advice of the Judicial Committee be taken, the Leader of the House, Mr Butler, had emphasised in the debate on the first report of the Committee of Privileges that the House would not regard itself as bound to accept that advice. Since

1. *In re Parliamentary Privilege Act, 1770* [1958], AC 331–54.

the Judicial Committee had refrained from expressing any views on the main question in issue—namely whether Mr Strauss's letter was a 'proceeding in Parliament', and whether legal proceedings in respect of it were in breach of the House's privileges—it now fell to the House to decide whether action should be taken against the London Electricity Board. A second report from the Committee of Privileges recommended that since the case was the first to arise out of the sending of a letter by a Member to a Minister, and since no legal proceedings had in fact been instituted, further action should not be taken against the Board. The Board in its turn later announced that it had decided not to proceed with legal action against Mr Strauss and had asked the Minister of Power to set up an independent inquiry[1] into the disputed facts contained in Mr Strauss's letter. The conclusion of the Committee of Privileges, that letters written by Members in the circumstances raised by the Strauss case should enjoy absolute privilege as 'proceedings in Parliament', remained, however, as an issue of principle upon which the House had yet to express its view. The debate on the Committee of Privileges' second report took place on 8 July 1958. Moving that the Committee's Report should be accepted, the Home Secretary said that the majority of the Committee had felt that in the light of modern circumstances a letter from a Member to a Minister about the administration of a nationalised industry might properly be regarded as a 'proceeding in Parliament'. Members would have to choose whether to support the Committee in this conclusion or to rely upon the ordinary law of qualified privilege which in the absence of malice would protect a Member forwarding a constituent's letter. Mr Herbert Morrison, arguing for the rejection of the Committee's Report, again urged that, in writing to Ministers, Members ought to find it possible to be circumspect in their language. The extension of absolute privilege to a letter sent privately to a Minister might work grave injustice to people outside. Speeches in the House could be answered. Where the privacy of the post was used, an injured individual had no means of knowing what had been said, and would have no legal remedy. On a free vote Mr Morrison's view prevailed and the Committee's Report was rejected by 218 votes to 213. 204 Government supporters (including the Attorney-General and the Government Whips), 13 Labour Members, and one Liberal voted against the Report. The minority supporting the Committee included the Home Secretary, the Leader of the Opposition, 180 Labour Members, and 28 Conservatives.

1. This inquiry did in fact exonerate the Board (Cmnd. 605, 1958).

The House's decision has been both applauded and condemned. It may be viewed alternatively as a breaking in of commonsense after a period of over-exuberant assertions of privilege by the Commons, or as a dangerous relaxation of the rights of Members as guardians of administrative propriety in the body politic. Some Members have, out of abundant caution, declined to take action on constituents' complaints. On 14 July 1958, Mr Nabarro stated that he had felt obliged to decline to pass on complaints about the operations of British Railways, and in letters to *The Times* several Members stressed the difficulty of checking defamatory allegations made in constituents' letters. The Speaker stated on 30 July 1958 that the Clerks at the Table would no longer follow the practice of advising Members to write to Ministers or Boards of Nationalised Industries. This was not intended, he added, to convey any advice against the writing of letters, and no doubt Members would use their discretion as hitherto. It is of course arguable that letters to outside bodies ought to be regarded differently from letters to Ministers who are Members of the House. During questions to the Minister of Health Members also suggested that in supplying details of complaints about the operation of the National Health Service they would be in danger of defaming individual physicians. The Speaker's opinion, however, was that where, on a matter arising out of a question on the order paper, a Member supplied written information to a Minister, the question and correspondence could be regarded as within the ambit of parliamentary proceedings.

The phrase 'proceeding in Parliament' is not, in fact, one which has ever been authoritatively construed by a court of law in this context. From the practice of the House, however, and from litigation involving its privileges, a number of deductions can be made. The primary form of proceeding in which Members are protected is, of course, speaking and voting. Not all words spoken in the House appear to come within this protection. Words exchanged between Members in the chamber, but not related to the business of the House, might provide an example, although there is no English authority on this point. On the other hand 'proceedings' are not confined to speaking and voting. The actions of officers of the House in pursuance of its orders are part of the House's proceedings. An assault upon or removal of a Member by the Sergeant-at-Arms would seem to be a 'proceeding' for this purpose.[1] Criminal acts within the walls of the House, but not connected with the proceedings of the House or done in pursuance of its instructions, are in principle

1. *Bradlaugh v. Gossett* [1884] 12 QBD 271 at 276.

amenable to the ordinary law. But to what extent the House can by express or implied authorisation make into a part of its 'proceedings' actions not directly connected with its legislative and deliberative business and which might otherwise be illegal is a more speculative matter. (The result, for example, of *R. v. Graham-Campbell* appears to be that the sale of alcohol within the precincts of the Commons outside statutorily permitted hours is properly described as a 'proceeding' of the House.)[1] Whether events taking place outside, or partly in and partly out of, the House can be treated as 'proceedings' because of a relation to the House's business is equally problematical. In 1939 a Select Committee of the House on the Official Secrets Acts[2] reported (and the House agreed) that the freedom of speech guaranteed in the Bill of Rights covered both the asking and the giving of written notice of a parliamentary question. This included, it was said, everything said or done by a Member in the exercise of his functions as a Member, either in committee or in the transaction of the business of the House—or, it seemed, outside the House. Though things done by a Member beyond the walls of Parliament would generally not be protected, the Committee continued: 'Cases may . . . easily be imagined of communications between one Member and another, or between a Member and a Minister, so closely related to some matter pending in or expected to be brought before the House, as for example where a Member sends to a Minister the draft of a question he is thinking of putting down or shows it to another Member with a view to obtaining advice as to the propriety of putting it down or as to the manner in which it should be framed.'

The Select Committee of 1939 cited a number of cases and opinions in support of the view that an act not done in the immediate presence of the House might yet be held to be done 'constructively' in Parliament. In a Canadian case, *R. v. Bunting* (1885), it was said that a Member was privileged and protected in respect of 'anything he may say or do within the scope of his duties in the course of parliamentary business'.[3] The Committee also noted two American decisions[4] on

1. See [1935] 1 KB 594. cf. Sir Alan Herbert's satirical *Crime in the Commons* based upon this decision. Members (it was suggested) 'can sell each other noxious drugs . . . they can play at Roulette in the Central Hall. . . . They can invite loose women to frequent the lobbies. . . . They can acquire firearms and assemble explosives without a licence. They can fight duals among themselves in the smoking-room or Crypt.' (*Uncommon Law*, pp. 420–1.)
2. HC 101 (1938–9). cf. *Report of the Committee of Privileges*, HC 146 (1938) on the case of Mr Sandys.
3. (1885) 7 Ontario Reports at 563.
4. *Coffin v. Coffin* 4 Mass 1, and *Kilbourn v. Thompson* 103 US 168.

the extent of constitutional provisions protecting the freedom of debate in legislative bodies, which suggested that privilege extended to 'every act resulting from the nature of the office of a Member and done in the execution of that office, whether done in the House or out of it'. The 1939 Committee Report quoted, in addition, the dictum of Lord Denman in *Stockdale v. Hansard* that 'all the privileges that can be required for the energetic discharge' by the Members of the House of their duties must be 'conceded without a murmur or a doubt'.[1]

Some of these formulations of the extent of 'proceedings in Parliament' are extremely wide, and it is not at all clear that they can be regarded as authoritative. They are also extremely difficult of application. Those dicta which turn around the concept of a Member of Parliament's 'duties' open a number of avenues of debate as to what those duties are. The dicta which invoke a connection between a matter physically external to the House and the possibility of its coming before the House by way of question, or in some other way, face the objection that practically anything is capable of coming before the House in some form or another.

Moreover, it cannot now be certain that the conclusions of the 1939 Committee represent the view of the House of Commons, for the House has now rejected the conclusion of its Committee of Privileges that Mr Strauss's letter was a 'proceeding in Parliament'. Since the Committee's findings in 1957 were based upon the dicta cited in 1939 it could be argued that the House has by resolution implicitly rescinded its earlier acceptance of these extremely wide propositions.

It remains true of course that whatever the Commons decides about the meaning of 'proceeding in Parliament' the courts may take a different view if called upon to decide the point in litigation. The Judicial Committee in its decision on the Parliamentary Privilege Act re-stated the constitutional dilemma which still exists in this sphere—namely that though the Commons view all matters pertaining to privilege as within their exclusive jurisdiction, the courts consider it their duty to decide according to their own interpretation of the law whether privilege exists. Only twentieth-century restraint prevents an irreconcilable deadlock between legislature and judiciary. The House has never formally relinquished the view which it expressed strongly in 1837 that the institution of legal proceedings in the courts for the purpose of questioning its privileges is itself a breach of privilege which renders all parties concerned liable to punishment. Parliamen-

1. 9 Ad. & El at 115.

tary Privilege thus remains a potentially live political issue. For the future, two developments—the increasing amount of political commentary and debate on television and the possibility of an acceptance of televised parliamentary proceedings—carry with them the likelihood of new and intriguing conflicts of interest.[1]

1. For some recent episodes see C. Seymour Ure, 'Parliamentary Privilege and Broadcasting', *Parliamentary Affairs* (1963), p. 411.

In August 1966 a Select Committee on Broadcasting of Proceedings in the House of Commons reported in favour of televising proceedings on a closed circuit for an experimental period, but the proposal was narrowly defeated. The implications for Parliamentary Privilege are discussed in paras 41–7 of the Report and in two memoranda by the Clerk of the House and the Attorney-General (Appendices 37 and 38), (HC 146, 1966).

In 1967 the report appeared of a Select Committee appointed to carry out a wide-ranging survey of Parliamentary Privilege (HC 34, 1967). The Report rejected proposals submitted to the Committee for a codification of contempts and for transfer of the Houses' jurisdication in this field to a judicial tribunal. (cf. Evidence of the Study of Parliament Group at p. 187 of the Report, and 'Penal Rights Preserved: the Select Committee on Parliamentary Privilege (1968), *Political Quarterly*, p. 219.)

8

MINISTERIAL RESPONSIBILITY: NOTES AND DEVELOPMENTS

In an informal, uncodified constitution like the British, what are, on the face of it, minor episodes, opinions, and pieces of vocabulary often assume an interest which might otherwise be lacking in a more precisely formulated system. They often illustrate uncertainties in existing and accepted principles, and provide the material from which arguments develop about the exact application of these principles. This is particularly true of the principle of ministerial responsibility with which we have been largely concerned. The miscellaneous points which follow may therefore be worth a slightly expanded note on one ground or the other.

1. *Deputy Prime Minister*

Institutions are sometimes said to be unknown either to the law or to the Constitution. In the first case the criteria are more obvious than the second. Sir Ivor Jennings has pointed out that the conventional office of Prime Minister is known to the law in that it is mentioned in at least three statutes—the Ministers of the Crown Act, 1937, the Chequers Estate Act, 1917, and the Physical Training and Recreation Act, 1937. The office of Deputy Prime Minister is a good example of an institution which it is sometimes suggested is 'unknown to the Constitution'—though it is not entirely clear what is meant by the phrase. Mr Attlee was certainly said to have acted in the capacity during the Second World War. Sir Winston Churchill writes of him as being in 1941 'now generally recognised as deputy Prime Minister'.[1] Mr Herbert Morrison was also known by this title in Mr Attlee's administration of 1945–50. Nevertheless King George VI, according to his biographer, remonstrated with Sir Winston for describing Mr Anthony Eden as 'Secretary of State for Foreign Affairs and Deputy Prime Minister' in his list of Cabinet Ministers in 1951. Sir John

1. *The Grand Alliance*, p. 425.

Wheeler-Bennett writes of 'the tendency on the part of the Prime Minister to appoint Ministers to constitutionally non-existent offices'. The King 'at once noticed this irregularity and on his instructions the latter title was deleted from Mr Eden's appointment'.[1] Wheeler-Bennett adds that recognition of any such title is highly undesirable as implying a restriction upon the Sovereign's unfettered choice of the Prime Minister's successor, in the event of death or resignation. It is not easy to see why any stronger fetter is implied than by, for example, Sir Winston's formal advice to the King in 1945 (submitted on the King's request) that Mr Eden should be sent for in the event of his own death and Sir John Anderson in the event of the deaths of both himself and Eden. The force of these transactions must of course be considered in relation to their wartime context.

In December 1956 Mr R. A. Butler was asked whether in view of the Prime Minister's absence abroad he would appoint an acting or deputy Prime Minister. Mr Butler replied that all necessary arrangements had been made to carry on the Queen's Government and that 'the office of deputy Prime Minister is not known to our constitution'.[2] In 1963, however, he himself assumed this dubiously respectable title.

2. *Responsibility for Dissolution and Prerogative Acts*

In 1955 the date fixed for the holding of the General Election coincided with that of the annual General Assembly of the Church of Scotland. The Moderator of the General Assembly appears to have protested to the Prime Minister about the inconvenience caused in Scotland by this particular date, and Mr Emrys Hughes attempted to question Sir Anthony Eden on the subject. His question was ruled to be out of order on the ground that the Prime Minister is not responsible to Parliament for advice given to the Crown about the dissolution of Parliament and the holding of a General Election.

Dissolution appears to be one of a small number of subjects clearly within the Government's responsibility but anomalously shielded from parliamentary questioning. The advice given to the Crown about the conferment of honours and about reprieves in capital cases provides other examples. On the other hand many governmental and legislative acts also take the form of advice to the Crown without precluding the parliamentary questioning of Ministers upon them.

3. *'Grand inquest of the nation'*

Parliament is often described as the 'grand inquest of the nation' but

1. *King George VI: His Life and Reign* (1958), p. 797.
2. 561 HC Deb., 5s., cs. 1448–9.

the origins of the phrase seem to be slightly obscure. It occurs in parliamentary oratory and occasionally in judicial proceedings. An example of the latter kind is to be found in Mr Justice Patteson's concurring judgment in *Stockdale v. Hansard.* The House of Commons, though not capable of making law by its resolutions, was 'the grand inquest of the nation, and [might] inquire into all alleged abuses and misconduct in any quarter'.[1] Macaulay, in reporting the arguments used against the trying of an offender at the bar of the House when proceeding by attainder, contrasted the procedure with trial in the ordinary courts where a judge if partial might be 'called to account by the great inquest of the nation'.[2] The context of the phrase in the eighteenth century is usually that of impeachment. Burke, on the impeachment of Warren Hastings, referred to the Commons as 'the greatest inquest of the nation'. Blackstone too introduces the description in his chapter 'Of Courts of Criminal Jurisdiction'. The impeachment of 'great and enormous offenders' before the Lords is a 'presentiment . . . by the most solemn grand inquest of the whole kingdom'.[3] 'Great inquest' is a term sometimes applied to the Domesday inquiry. Often it appears to have been used as a description of a local body such as a grand jury. At some point it was applied by analogy to the Members of the centralised representative body. 'The lower house or Representative of the Commons' is described in a work published in 1671 as 'a Court of grand Enquest to exhibit the grievances of the Nation and the People who did choose them to represent them'.[4]

4. *Government policy and party policy*

There are some difficulties, both linguistic and practical, in distinguishing party policy and governmental policy. The distinction between 'government' in the sense of continuing legal organs and machinery and 'government' in the sense of the administration in office at any one time is not one which is marked in English by any easy verbal convention. 'State' perhaps would suffice for the former, but it is hardly a received term of art in this country. In law it must mean the Crown and that is too narrow an idea to stand for the entity which in non-legal conversation is indicated by 'state'. 'State' is also frequently used in a wider sense for the community as a whole

1. [1839] 9 Ad. & El at 193.
2. *History of England*, vol. 4, p. 748.
3. IV *Commentaries* (5th ed.), p. 259.
4. Fabian Phillips, *Regale Necessarium:* or *the Legality, Reason and Necessity of the Rights and Privileges justly claimed by the King's Servants; and which ought to be allowed unto them.*

considered as an international entity. 'The Public' (as Maitland noted) makes certain appearances in the statute book and the public policy which is laid down in the courts might be described as state policy in that it has been judicially distinguished from the political or legislative policy of any particular government.[1] Between the public offices which politicians hold and their private and party personalities we do have a clear notional separation. The Prime Minister may broadcast to the nation in his capacity as Government spokesman as distinct from his capacity as party leader. The idea, however, that there might be non-party broadcasts or statements by Her Majesty's Leader of the Opposition in his official constitutional as distinct from his party capacity is one which has not been advanced. Perhaps this brings out the point that with policies as distinct from persons the separation between the governmental and the political is more difficult. That 'in a great many matters the distinction between Government policy and the policy of the party in power has no practical force' was a conclusion reached by *The Times* in December 1958, commenting upon the result of an inquiry into an allegation that Government publicity facilities had been used for the circulation of political propaganda. In this instance the suggestion was unfounded.[2] (A directive subsequently issued to departments stated that official mailing lists should not be made available to outside organisations engaging in politically controversial activity and that the texts of Ministers' speeches should be distributed by official machinery only when made on official occasions.) But quite apart from any question of abuse the distinction within the operations of the Central Office of Information and the Press sections of government departments between information and advocacy is not always obvious. In principle the criteria for both national ministerial broadcasting (as distinct from party controversial broadcasting) and for government information activities have been laid down in a roughly similar way. They are that such expositions should be factual and explanatory of legislative or administrative policies or in the nature of appeals to the nation to co-operate in national policies. But if legislation is the subject of political controversy or if (as at the time of the Suez intervention of 1956) there is no accepted national policy, then uncontroversial application of the principles is impossible (and most obviously so in broadcasting information overseas).

Modern methods of publicity may increase these difficulties. In March 1958, for example, Opposition Members of Parliament

1. *Monkland v. Jack Barclay Ltd.* [1951] 2 KB 252 at 265.

2. Cmnd. 583 (1958). cf. *The Times*, 13 November 1958. The allegations concerned the misuse of OHMS address labels. cf. HC Deb., 19 July 1971.

questioned the Prime Minister about the appearance on commercial television of the Chief Information Officer of the Treasury. Mr Herbert Morrison complained that the Government had made a serious departure from existing principles which might weaken the impartiality and special character of the Civil Service. Mr Macmillan defended the practice of factual statements by Civil Servants. The rules governing such appearances had been laid down by Treasury circular in February 1956. He conceded, however, that between the extremes of political propaganda and of broadcasts by Civil Service meteorologists of the daily weather report expressions of opinion of a non-factual kind might occur.[1]

In May 1958 the Prime Minister answered further questions about the alleged involvement in politics of one of the service departments —by way not so much of exposition but of opposition to government policy. The views of the Air Staff on defence policy were expounded and made public at a meeting ('Conference Prospect') to which a number of Members of Parliament were invited. The Leader of the Opposition argued that it was not desirable that departmental points of view which were not those of the Government should be propounded in this way. This view of the matter was not universal. One academic critic[2] was willing to hail the experiment as a constitutional advance which might allow the public to make a more informed assessment of the divergent views on policy normally concealed behind the curtain of ministerial responsibility, and in addition provide Civil Servants with an alternative to the dilemma of obedience or resignation where differences about policy raised serious moral and political issues.

5. *Judicial criticism of Ministers and Parliament*

The well-known (and variously viewed) dissent of Lord Atkin in *Liversidge v. Anderson*[3] contained some extremely strong words about the attitude of the Bench to Ministers' powers. He viewed, it will be remembered, 'with apprehension the attitude of judges who on a mere question of construction, when face to face with claims involving the liberty of the subject, show themselves more executive-minded than the executive. . . . In this case,' he added, 'I have listened to arguments which might have been addressed acceptably to the Court of King's Bench in the time of Charles I.' Lord Atkin's daughter has recently related that this passage was not favourably received by his

1. 584 HC Deb., 5s., c. 1091. The Treasury Circular is appended in full in *Hansard* (cs. 1093–6).
2. Brian Chapman (*Manchester Guardian*, 14 May 1958).
3. [1942] AC 206.

colleagues and that he was asked to omit it from his judgment, but refused to do so.[1] In reporting the decision, the editor of the *Law Quarterly Review*, Dr A. L. Goodhart, suggested that his journal might have been guilty of contempt if in commenting on the decision they had endorsed Lord Atkin's views. Luckily the editorial opinion favoured the construction adopted by the majority of their Lordships. Criticism of judicial attitudes from the Bench is certainly less common in this country than in the United States. The same might be said of judicial criticism of Parliament. Though of course no question of invalidation can arise, to what extent are judges entitled to comment adversely upon the policy of the legislature? The convention would appear to be that criticism of Parliament's handiwork is permissible provided that undue reflection is not cast upon the policy behind the statute—a distinction not always easy to maintain. Lord Denning has made some extra-judicial suggestions on the point. 'The true principle, as I understand it, is that judges are entitled to make responsible comments or suggestions on the way in which Acts work if it appears to them necessary to do so in the public interest . . . subject to the qualification that judges must never comment in disparaging terms on the policy of Parliament, for that would be to cast reflections on the wisdom of Parliament. . . . Just as Members of Parliament must not cast reflections on the judges, so judges must not cast reflections on the conduct of Parliament.'[2]

Members of Parliament are in fact much more restricted in one sense than the general public. Though shielded by their parliamentary immunity from the risks of contempt on an occasion when a substantive motion relating to judicial conduct is before the House, they cannot within the rules of order on any other occasion cast even the most indirect reflection upon the integrity of judges either in particular or in general. The rule if strictly applied is perhaps over-narrow. It was invoked in 1912 when Mr Lansbury suggested that the fortunes of Mrs Pankhurst and Mrs Lawrence in court had been influenced by the agitation and pressure of their friends in society.[3] A Member who wished to draw attention to what he felt to be the undesirability of judges in Scotland holding directorships in trading companies was held to have identified certain judges by his references and to have infringed the rule.[4] References of an even more general character to the judicial mind and its alleged merits or failings may also perhaps be impermissible. Mr Winston Churchill was challenged

1. *Some Memories of Lord Atkin* (GLIM, Summer 1957), p. 13.
2. 29 *Canadian Bar Review* (1951), 1193.
3. 61 HC Deb., 5s., c. 2779.
4. 91 HC Deb., 5s., c. 664.

on a point of order when as Home Secretary in 1911 he wished to criticise the decision in the *Osborne* case of 1909 which adversely affected the pursuit by trade unions of political objects. In such cases, he argued, where political, class, and party interests were involved, the courts did not command universal confidence and a very large number of the population had, he felt, been led to the view that the courts were, 'no doubt unconsciously, biassed'.[1] The Deputy Speaker considered these remarks to be a reflection upon 'the general body of judges'.

In the Commonwealth the application of British conventions in this sphere may sometimes raise difficult issues. In the Union of South Africa, for example, between 1952 and 1956, the correctness of decisions taken by the Supreme Court was a matter of heated political difference between Government and Opposition and it was extremely difficult to apply the Speaker's ruling (referring to Todd's *Parliamentary Government in England*) that the House must accept in its debates that legal decisions were correct. Even when legislation to vary the effect of a legal decision was before the House, Members, it was held, should not question its correctness in law, though they might freely discuss its consequences.[2] Are Members of the House of Commons in the same position? And may the Lords properly question in debate the correctness of decisions made by them in their judicial capacity?

6. *The Law Officers and ministerial responsibility*

There is one species of Minister whose responsibilities *vis-à-vis* Parliament and their colleagues exemplify both the uncertain nature of constitutional conventions and the delicacy of the distinction between the policy of the Government of the day and the policy of the state. This is the Attorney-General, along with his deputy the Solicitor-General and their Scottish counterparts. Their powers, it is felt, must be exercised in a non-political way, without heed to potential pressure or clamour. Yet their activity or lack of it may sometimes be of acute political and parliamentary interest. In 1956 the Foreign Office drew attention to their status when it informed the Soviet Chargé d'Affaires that the Government were unable to intervene to withdraw a prosecution against a Russian athlete, Madame Nina Ponomareva, charged with shoplifting whilst on a visit to London. It had been pointed out, *The Times* reported, that the Attorney-General was in no sense an agent of the Government.[3] The exact

1. 26 HC Deb., 5s., c. 1022.
2. 82 House of Assembly Deb. 2156–7 (1953).
3. *The Times*, 28 September 1958.

degree of the Attorney-General's independence of the political process and the conclusions which are to be drawn from it do not, however, seem to be established in particularly sharp detail. The question of cabinet membership may illustrate this point. It has often been suggested that the Attorney-General ought to be 'the adviser but not a part of the executive'.[1] Yet the Law Officers are Ministers and collectively responsible along with their colleagues for the actions of the executive. The question seems often to have been settled by considerations of political prestige rather than constitutional nicety. In 1912 Sir Rufus Isaacs was given a seat in Mr Asquith's cabinet (as a consolation prize for the Woolsack). Sir John Simon, Sir Edward Carson, and F. E. Smith also had cabinet rank. The last-named in fact became Lord Chancellor Birkenhead as the result of (or at least after) refusing to continue as Attorney-General in Lloyd George's reconstructed ministry of 1919 without cabinet membership. Lord Simon, however, has expressed in his Memoirs the view that the combination of offices is, if not improper, at least undesirable as making it difficult for the Attorney-General to approach his task of giving legal advice to the Government with an open mind.[2] One of his successors in office, Sir Hartley Shawcross, has expressed a similar opinion, namely that 'the independence and detachment of his office should not be blurred by his inclusion in the political body, the cabinet which may have to take decisions on policy after receiving the legal advice that the Law Officers may give'.[3] In the course of representing the public interest the Attorney-General may also be faced, when an inquiry is instituted under the Tribunals of Inquiry (Evidence) Act of 1921, with subjecting one or more of his ministerial colleagues to public cross-examination. Both Sir Hartley Shawcross and Sir Reginald Manningham-Buller have discharged this duty (before the Lynskey Tribunal of 1948 and the Parker Tribunal of 1957). How it could be discharged in the event of an inquiry into matters of a more political nature, for which the Attorney-General might share responsibility, is less clear.[4]

There is an equal uncertainty about the nature of the Law Officers' responsibility to Parliament. They are, in Anson's words, 'Members of the House of Commons and responsible to Parliament for the advice given to the Crown and its servants'.[5] Yet questions to Ministers about the advice given by the Law Officers are out of order

1. Birkenhead: *Frederick Edwin, Earl of Birkenhead* (1935), p. 112.
2. *Retrospect. The Memoirs of the Rt Hon Viscount Simon* (1952), p. 90.
3. 'The Office of the Attorney-General', *Parliamentary Affairs* (1953–4), p. 383.
4. See *Royal Commission on Tribunals of Inquiry* (1966), Cmnd. 3121, p. 33.
5. *Law and Custom of the Constitution* (4th ed. 1935), vol. 2, pt. 1, pp. 221–2.

in the Commons. Erskine May treats such advice as being amongst the class of matters in their nature secret and confidential. Civil Servants are said to be not responsible to Parliament precisely because they are in a position to give confidential advice to Ministers. What then is the difference between being responsible and not being responsible here except that Law Officers are part of a Ministry and may fall with it. They certainly share the collective responsibility of the Government but Anson's statement appears to relate to individual responsibility.

There seems to have been some impression in the minds of Members of Parliament on certain occasions not merely that Ministers could not be compelled by question to reveal the Law Officers' opinions but that it was constitutionally improper for them to do so voluntarily. In 1858 when the opinions of the Law Officers on a point of international law were laid before the House it was stated that an exception was being made from a 'settled rule that neither the papers laid before those officers nor the opinions which they gave founded upon them should be communicated to Parliament'.[1] In 1865 Sir Robert Peel was interrupted on a point of order as he was about to read an opinion of the Irish Attorney-General. The Speaker ruled that the practice was not contrary to any Order of the House,[2] and Lord Palmerston argued that there were occasions when disclosure was convenient and proper, but that the general rule allowed the Law Officers to give frank advice without the caution which might be induced by a knowledge that their views were to be laid before the House. The point is understandable but it hardly chimes with the idea of responsibility. A somewhat different basis for the alleged rule was suggested in 1913—namely that Ministers themselves must be responsible both for the wisdom and the legality of their actions. They cannot, it was argued, 'in the least degree shift their responsibility by accepting the opinion of the Law Officers of the Crown on any matter whatsoever'.[3] On this occasion the Speaker stated the position to be that neither the Law Officers nor Ministers could be called upon to say what was in the opinions furnished, but that there was no objection to asking a Minister whether he had taken the Law Officers' advice, and that was frequently done. It seems extremely uncertain whether there is any convention that opinions ought to be confidential. Lord MacDermott has written that 'the present constitutional practice is not to publish or rest upon contemporary opinions'. A Minister cannot, he adds, defend himself from criticism by saying

1. 149 Parlt. Deb., 3s., cs. 101, 178.
2. 177 Parlt. Deb., 3s., c. 354.
3. 46 HC Deb., 5s. (Mr Swift McNeil).

that he wanted to take a certain course of action but that the Attorney-General would not let him.[1] It might of course be more delicate to say that the law would not let him, but certainly Ministers do on occasion make the views of the Law Officers a part of their arguments and those views may often be tested or questioned in the general course of debates in which the Attorney-General or Solicitor-General are taking part. Here the obligations of the Law Officers to defend the legality of government action, and their duties as servants of the state and advisers of the House of Commons,[2] might seem to be potentially in conflict. The last of these aspects appears most clearly in questions such as those arising from parliamentary privilege. In 1957–8 the Attorney-General's views in this sphere differed from those of some of his ministerial colleagues and from those of a majority of the Committee of Privileges.

The tension between the governmental and state capacities of the Attorney-General appears perhaps in its sharpest form when his control over the machinery of justice has to be exercised in cases politically embarrassing to the Government. In summary proceedings, as the Foreign Office implies in its 1956 statement, a prosecution once instituted can be withdrawn only with the leave of the court, but in more serious cases on indictment. It is undeniable that a discretion in relation to the withdrawal of proceedings rests with the Attorney-General. Ought he to exercise it as a Government servant or in the light of the public interest as he himself sees it? Views which have been expressed by holders of the office and by Ministers do not all seem to be reconcilable. Prosecutions for offences having a political aspect may of course involve the reputations of Ministers and engage the attention of the Cabinet. Nevertheless when the War Cabinet during the First World War instructed the Attorney-General to institute certain proceedings Sir Frederick Smith refused to act until (according to a later account of Sir Patrick Hastings) the 'unconstitutional minute' had been excised.[3] Sir Patrick Hastings's own difficulties in the matter of the Campbell prosecution, which brought down the Labour Government of 1924, revealed, however, certain differences of view within the House of Commons.[4] The withdrawal of the prosecution of the Communist editor of the *Workers' Weekly* led to an Opposition demand for an inquiry into suggestions that the

1. *Protection from Power under English Law*, p. 30.

2. The law officers are also constitutional advisers to the House of Lords, to which they were originally summoned by writs similar to those of the judges. These writs are still issued (see 206 *House of Lords' Debates* 377–82, 19 November 1957) but now ignored (Edwards *The Law Officers of the Crown*, 1964, p. 4).

3. 177 HC Deb., 5s., c. 614.

4. 177 HC Deb., 5s., cs. 10, 598–629.

proceedings had been withdrawn as the result of political representations by Labour Members of Parliament. A parliamentary question to the Attorney-General asking whether he had communicated with certain members was disallowed privately by the Speaker. In the House Sir Patrick Hastings explained that the decision to withdraw was entirely his own although he was acquainted with the views of the Cabinet. This, he argued, was entirely appropriate, though his remarks seem to be directed to two rather different conclusions—one, that his public duty might differ from his political duty, and secondly that his public duty was in fact to be guided by the political views of the executive in matters of public policy. If, he argued, the public interest conflicted with the strict exercise of his duty in a matter such as sedition, the Attorney-General would be justified in going to the Government and asking whether prosecution were desirable. Lord Hewart in 1919 had so interpreted his duty, believing that the question was one for Ministers. Mr Ramsay MacDonald agreed with his Attorney-General that in prosecutions of a political character the opinion of the Law Officers might legitimately be altered or influenced by the executive. The opinions he had expressed to the Attorney-General, he added, had not been conveyed as mandatory instructions and were not of a personal or party nature. Sir John Simon seemed to hold a divergent view. The discretion of the executive in instituting and withdrawing prosecutions was, he suggested, conceded on the plain basis that it should be exercised without intervention by the Prime Minister. Mr Baldwin, succeeding Mr MacDonald as Prime Minister, admitted in answer to a parliamentary question by his predecessor that the Attorney-General should, when public policy was involved, inform himself of the views of appropriate Ministers as factors which might affect his decision. Instructions laid down by the Labour Government had, however, been rescinded since they went beyond that.[1] It may be noted that when the regulations laid down for the Director of Public Prosecutions by the Attorney-General were revised in 1946 a reference to 'cases where an order . . . is given to the Director by the Secretary of State' was omitted.

Some categorical statements about the position of the Law Officers were made in February 1959 when the Commons set up a Tribunal of Inquiry to investigate allegations of assault against two Scottish police constables. No prosecution had been instituted, but the Prime Minister felt that it would be improper either for instructions on the matter to be given to the Scottish Law Officers or for their conduct to be included within the scope of the inquiry. To issue instructions would be to err against 'the first rule a Cabinet owed to

1. 179 HC Deb., 5s., c. 1214.

the Law Officers'. Mr Macmillan added that he did not 'want a Campbell case in reverse'. In view of the importance attached to the withdrawal of the Campbell prosecution in 1924 it is important to decide whether as a precedent it does establish what is frequently attributed to it. It may be necessary to distinguish two propositions which if loosely expressed may become confused. One is that no decision of the Law Officers may properly be influenced by party political pressure or by considerations primarily affecting the electoral standing of the Government. It does not follow merely from this that in no circumstances ought the Attorney-General to be influenced or instructed by the Government on a matter of public policy, or subjected to parliamentary inquisition on his actions. This was the view that MacDonald and Hastings took in the House in 1924 and the defeat of the Labour administration does not not demonstrate that they were wrong. It could be more accurately said to reflect suspicion that the Prime Minister's evasive explanations concealed party pressure for withdrawal, and reflected also the Opposition parties' disinclination to believe that such back-bench pressure had not been decisive.

The type of case in which the Cabinet's views on public policy may be relevant is not of course easy to define. What are commonly called 'political' cases or prosecutions do not come ready-labelled. Prosecutions for sedition, breaches of the Official Secrets Act and the like are plainly political. But any type of case may acquire political significance by attracting public attention or for other extraneous reasons. In all this the Attorney-General is caught between two theories. A part of him is an embodiment of the State and should, it seems implied, function as a kind of windowless monad, responsible to nobody. Yet he is also collectively responsible with his colleagues for his views on public policy. Clearly, if in a confusion of precedents the Law Officers are to be thought of as exercising exclusively independent and non-political functions, it would be undesirable if not improper to exercise political control or to suggest answerability to the House—as it would be to subject to political inquisition a judge or tribunal whose findings had aroused popular indignation. It is precisely because the Law Officers do, as things stand, exercise a governmental, administrative, or political discretion that they are properly answerable for their uses of it to the legislature, along with policemen and cabinet ministers. For Parliament to exercise its control by means of a tribunal of inquiry is preferable in obvious ways to exercising it by defeating a Government, as it defeated MacDonald. There would have been nothing constitutionally improper in including the actions of the Law Officers in the terms of reference of such an inquiry as that into the Waters allegations in 1959. It is not entirely satisfactory that Parliament should be faced with a choice between half an inquisitorial loaf, as in 1959, or no bread, as in 1924.

7. *Opposition responsibility*

Some conflicting ideas about the respective responsibilities of Government and Opposition were broached in March and April of 1958 when approaches were made by the Prime Minister to the Leader of the Opposition envisaging the possibility of joint talks between himself and Mr Gaitskell on defence matters. The suggestion was declined, and it was suggested that the arrangement was incompatible with the fulfilment by the Opposition of its constitutional function of criticism. The imparting of confidential information to Opposition leaders might clearly in many circumstances place them in an inhibiting and embarrassing position in relation to back-bench members of the Opposition party. Both party leaders, however, were in agreement that the disclosing of information to a Committee of the House was not an alternative which they were prepared to support.

A number of arguments were advanced in criticism of these attitudes. Amongst them was the suggestion[1] that the Opposition has a responsibility to the Crown which cannot be discharged if information which would aid them in their duties is refused, and that the duties of the Opposition could not be construed as merely being to oppose until such time as a change of government took place. It was urged in addition that the leaders of parties in office are frequently in possession of information which they cannot disclose to their followers and that the ultimate responsibility of Ministers for the advice given to the Crown would not in this sphere be fatally undermined by consultation or even 'the educative device of a special Parliamentary Committee'.[2] What could or would be disclosed to such a committee clearly depends more upon the particular degree of mutual trust between party leaders at any one time than upon constitutional convention. The absence of consultation in October 1956 was not caused by the lack of an appropriate parliamentary forum for it.

The case for advisory committees of the House which might receive information and advice from Ministers (who would be *ex officio* members) was placed before the Select Committees on Procedure which reported in 1959 and 1965. The case was argued in 1957–9 in relation to a Committee on Colonial Affairs. Though it was not

1. Professor Max Beloff (*The Times*, 29 April 1958).
2. ibid.

suggested that the proposed Committee should have any executive power the majority of the Select Committee rejected the idea on the ground that its activity 'would ultimately be aimed at controlling rather than criticising the policy and actions of the departments concerned'.[1] Opponents of advisory committees have, it may be noted, rejected them both as derogating from the authority of the House as a whole and also of unreasonably augmenting it.

8. *'Overlords' and ministerial responsibility*

The dispute in 1951–2 about the merits of co-ordinating Ministers provided an excellent and somewhat extended example of the potential confusion which is inherent in the concept of 'responsibility'. Controversy was raised principally by the announcement in October 1951 that Lord Woolton and Lord Leathers were to act as co-ordinators, on the one hand of Food and Agriculture, and on the other of Transport, Fuel, and Power. The appointments were attacked by the Opposition on the constitutional ground that the clarity of the individual responsibility of Ministers to Parliament had been compromised. Mr Attlee in November 1951 argued that Ministers who co-ordinated in a publicly announced capacity were 'apt to take away responsibility from the Departmental Minister'. Mr Herbert Morrison in the following year, and in his book *Government and Parliament*, repeated the criticism. The functions of co-ordination exercised during the war by the chairmen of Cabinet committees were, he thought, to be differentiated. They were a domestic arrangement which he and Sir John Anderson had felt should operate in secrecy. But the 'overlords' had specific responsibilities which would 'move the responsibilities away from departmental Ministers'.[2] The noble Lords, it was added, were not available for questioning in the Commons and their spheres of responsibility were insufficiently defined.

Whatever the merits of the 'overlords' as an administrative device (the experiment did not extend beyond 1953), a fairly general opinion seems to have been that the constitutional objections put forward by the Opposition were well founded. But the reasoning behind the criticisms may perhaps be questioned. In what sense did the existence of Lords Woolton and Leathers 'move the responsibilities away'—in Mr Morrison's phrase—from the departmental Ministers? 'Responsibilities' in the sense of duties personally discharged may well have diminished. That would not in itself seem to be, from the constitutional point of view, any concern of the Opposi-

1. HC 92 (1959), p. xxv. But see further below pp. 146–9.
2. 493 HC Deb., 5s., cs. 834–5. cf. *Government and Parliament* (1954), pp. 45–52.

tion or the Commons. 'Responsibility' in the sense of the ability of a departmental Minister to make a whole-hearted or convincing defence of a policy not entirely of his own making may also have diminished. But that phenomenon is merely part of a burden which all Ministers share from time to time as part of the consequences of the interdependence of the various parts of a government's policy. The fiscal action, for example, which a Chancellor of the Exchequer may be compelled to defend may be forced upon him by Prime Ministerial or cabinet decisions, and the fact be well known, without its normally being felt that the constitutional rights of the House are being prejudiced. When a junior Minister answers for his ministerial colleague there is not, unless some large policy issue is involved, any feeling that ministerial responsibility is being evaded by the mere fact that a parliamentary answer is being read by a Minister who has not personally taken the decision which the answer explains and defends. What the Opposition conventionally has a right to is that every aspect of the Government's activity which is actually discharged under the direction of Ministers should be explorable by parliamentary question; that questions should be answered by some Minister able to explain fully what has been done; and that the appropriate recipients for questions should be clearly designated. Some criticism on the last of these counts may perhaps have been justified in the early stages of Sir Winston Churchill's experiment. But the Prime Minister made in November 1951 a fairly detailed statement about the arrangements for putting down questions, and though it cannot be said that the Government's explanations of the actual hierarchical arrangements were consistently lucid, it is arguable that any such administrative embarrassments with which Ministers were faced as a result did not affect the rights of the House, any more than do the inner struggles of a Minister whom the doctrine of collective responsibility forces to prefer acquiescence to resignation. It is, in fact, sometimes felt to be a pleasing feature of Cabinet Government, making for governmental stability, that Ministers are compelled to defend, because of a general solidarity of policy, individual decisions which they may not have initiated or favoured. As the Prime Minister later emphasised, the departmental Ministers involved had access to the Cabinet and could resign if asked to carry out policies with which they could not agree. The co-ordinating Ministers, it may be noted, differed from the Minister of Defence set up in 1946 in that the latter's co-ordinating powers were defined by statute. The former were in a sense mere public monuments—perhaps unwisely unveiled —to the potential rigours of collective responsibility. It is difficult to agree that on the central point of their announced existence any constitutional objection could be made out, though politically and morally it may be important to feel able accurately to allocate praise and blame amongst Ministers.

9. *Ministerial refusal of information*

Both the individual and collective accountability of Ministers is tempered by the convention that any Minister may on grounds of public interest, or indeed on no specified ground at all, refuse to provide information in reply to a parliamentary question. In May 1956 Sir Anthony Eden referred to the 'long-established convention that a responsible Minister may decline to give information' in refusing to answer questions about the circumstances in which Commander Lionel Crabb, an ex-naval 'frogman', had met his death. It was widely surmised that Commander Crabb had been engaged in underwater espionage against two Russian cruisers in Portsmouth harbour. In the previous month the Admiralty had stated that the death had occurred in connection with the testing of underwater equipment. Sir Anthony in making his statement said: 'While it is the practice for Ministers to accept responsibility, I think it necessary, in the special circumstances of this case, to make it clear that what was done was done without the authority or the knowledge of her Majesty's Ministers. Appropriate disciplinary steps are being taken.'[1] Though pressed for more information he would not enlarge further and the Speaker ruled out of order a motion for the adjournment of the House.

The debate also showed that responsibility for the activites of the secret service is (not surprisingly) a somewhat elusive concept. Opposition Members attacked the Prime Minister for his 'complete evasion of responsibility'. Mr Gaitskell conceded that details of the activities of the secret service could not be given, but urged that Parliament's acceptance of a limitation of its control in this respect rested upon certain assumptions—namely that Ministers themselves should effectively control the services: that they should be in fact secret; that the activities in question should not embarrass the country's international relations; and that they should, as far as anyone could make out, be reasonably successful. In the present case none of these conditions appeared to have been fulfilled. If Ministers were not effectively in control it was the duty of Members to raise the matter. The decisions involved must have been known to the Admiralty. If they were taken at a high level irresponsibility existed which demanded criticism. If they were taken at a low level it indicated that the personnel involved had got out of hand and were

1. 552 HC Deb., 5s., c. 1220 and cs. 1760–4.

operating with a frightening degree of political unawareness. The Prime Minister in reply reiterated his refusal to discuss the points raised. This he believed was entirely in accord with our constitutional practice.[1] In domestic affairs there were many things which Ministers were not obliged to state publicly. The Home Secretary was not compelled to disclose the grounds on which he had decided to deport an alien or refused a certificate of naturalisation. Information was often concealed from the House in matters of defence. A classic example was the atomic bomb, where the whole expenditure of a hundred million pounds was concealed in the estimates for that particular year. Ministers did of course normally accept responsibility for the actions of officials. He had pondered long before departing from that axiom and had taken the exceptional step of making it plain that Ministers had not authorised what was done. His object was to ensure that no doubt should be thrown upon their sincerity in the discussions which they were conducting with the Russian leaders. In these circumstances, it is not easy to see what other course Sir Anthony could have taken. The hazards of candour in such matters have since been amply demonstrated in the United States.

10. *Suez and parliamentary accountability*

The political events of late 1956 impinged upon the Constitution at what might be described with some justification as its two most sensitive points—namely collective responsibility and party discipline. One consequence of the all-or-nothing responsibility of governments to the House of Commons is that there is a species of 'blind area' into which inquiry of a purely factual kind is unlikely to take place. Where charges of corruption or minor administrative scandal are in question there is a satisfactory forum of inquiry in the tribunals which may be set up under the Act of 1921. At the other end of the scale come accusations of a merely political kind for which the normal party conflict between Government and Opposition is the appropriate solvent. But in between there exists no obviously suitable body which can conduct an impartial inquiry into questions of fact or allegations of major administrative mismanagement upon which Ministers may wish for good or bad reasons to keep silent. In December 1958 Mr Harold Macmillan, in refusing Opposition demands for a Select Committee on the Suez operations and to inquire into charges of collusion in 1956 between Britain, France and Israel, replied that the verdict must be left 'to history and the electorate'—a view which, it was argued, minimised the difficulty of reaching verdicts in the absence of the evidence. One critic of the British

1. cf. the answers (19 July 1960) on espionage flights over the USSR.

military intervention of 1956 has adverted to the procedural difficulties which might arise if a parliamentary investigation[1] into any aspect of the events of that year were to be undertaken. For 'of the many weaknesses of modern British parliamentary government, the most glaring is the lack of inquisitory power'.[2] The Privy Councillors' oath of secrecy and the Official Secrets Acts are two of the possible obstacles mentioned. There is, however, a well-sanctioned procedure for obtaining the assent of the Crown to a disclosure of matters discussed in Cabinet. Anson states that the permission is normally obtained through the intervention of the Prime Minister. (Might it alternatively be obtained by a direct address of the Commons to the Crown?) The Official Secrets Act could hardly be invoked except on the initiative of the Law Officers. Do the Acts in any event bar disclosures to the Commons or to a Select Committee in the absence of the public? The weighting of a parliamentary Select Committee in favour of the majority party is more serious. It is not, however, fatal to the primary purpose of factual investigation provided that serious inquiry and a public record are achieved. A Select Committee of both Houses is perhaps the most appropriate instrument which the Constitution can muster for a purpose such as this.

A less satisfactory but possible alternative might be a Committee of Privy Councillors such as examined security procedures in 1955, and the tapping of telephones in 1957.

Any form of independent inquiry into major policy matters will naturally be resisted by Ministers on political grounds. Mr Gladstone, in 1855, seemed, however, prepared to assert that parliamentary inquisition into such matters was an infringement of constitutional propriety. Opposing the inquiry into the conduct of the Crimean War he argued that 'The judgment of the present Government belongs to a higher tribunal—I mean the enlightened opinion of the country.' Gladstone's view did not prevail and he was in any event prepared to concede the propriety of inquiry into a completed as distinct from a continuing operation—a concession perhaps inconsistent with his remark (echoed none the less in the 1950s) that judgment belonged to the electorate.

If Suez placed strains upon party loyalties in Westminster it also gave new point to old arguments about the responsibilities of

1. The parliamentary inquiry into the Jameson Raid provides a parallel of a lesser kind. Some of the procedure and its deficiency is well described in A. G. Gardiner's *Life of Sir William Harcourt* (1923), vol. 2, pp. 423 ff.

2. R. B. McCallum, 'The Flight to Liberalism', *Contemporary Review* (1958), p. 245.

Members to their local parties and constituents. Mr Nigel Nicolson has related in some detail[1] the predicament of a Member who found himself at issue both with his political leaders and his local constituency association. Placed in a similar situation by his support of the Government's action, one Labour Member (Mr Stanley Evans) resigned his seat. Eight Conservative Members in all abstained from supporting the Government in a vote of confidence. Within a month (in Mr Nicolson's words) 'one had resigned his seat in Parliament, one had become an Independent Member, one had previously announced his intention not to stand again, two had been ostracised by their constituency associations and two were in deep disgrace with theirs'.[2] Mr Nicolson, however, refused to resign his seat and was supported by the President of his constituency association. At a meeting of the Conservative Constituency Association of Bournemouth East and Christchurch Mr Nicolson made public a letter in which the President, Lord Quickswood, had expressed to him the view that no Member could properly be turned out of Parliament except by a vote of the House of Commons, and that, being a representative of the whole Commons of the Realm, he had done no wrong in voting against his party at the behest of his conscience. Nevertheless, the objects stated by Mr Nicolson himself do not appear to embrace this Burkeian extreme. They imply not a right to ignore the wishes of electors on particular issues but merely a wish to obtain a genuine expression of the wishes of a majority of his local party to be expressed at a secret ballot before the selection of a prospective parliamentary candidate. The right of a local party to select a candidate of its choice, he argues, implies the right to change him for another if he fails to satisfy them. Nevertheless there remains the question whether a constituency party ought to treat dissenting action on isolated occasions as conduct which fails to satisfy them. The difficulty is not merely that of distinguishing between isolated issues involving conscience and issues upon which loyalty to party leaders and the expectations of electors may be insisted upon. Issues of conscience are not necessarily trivial or non-political. In this instance they raised political issues of the first importance, which might in any constituency calculation be felt to outweigh a consistent conformity with party philosophy on a large number of other issues. There is indeed little tenable ground between the out-and-out view of Edmund Burke and that of the Bournemouth East constituency caucus; but if the conventions of the Constitution were to be codified

1. *People and Parliament* (1958), chs. 4–6.

2. Sir Robert Boothby, Mr Anthony Nutting, Sir Edward Boyle, Mr J. J. Astor, Sir Frank Medlicott, Colonel Banks, and Mr William Yates.

on the basis of current political practice there seems little doubt as to which of the two doctrines would qualify for inclusion.[1]

11. *Accountability and the interdependence of policy*

The traditional notion of a number of discrete ministerial responsibilities for which the respective office-holders are liable to give an account of themselves to the legislature is obviously threatened to the extent that departmental policies are interdependent. The 'overlord' arrangements of the early 1950s were received with perturbation by the Opposition. But the collectivisation of departmental responsibilities has become increasingly obvious in a number of important fields of policy. Economic, foreign and colonial, and defence policies provide examples. The formal individual responsibilities of the Service Ministers to Parliament do not represent distinct spheres of administration for which they alone are responsible, since their decisions are determined in many respects by the policy laid down by the Minister of Defence (who in turn is not acting independently of the Cabinet). The responsibilities of the Colonial and Commonwealth Relations Offices may sometimes be no easier to disentangle, and the sphere of action of the Foreign Secretary is increasingly circumscribed by and dependent upon Prime Ministerial activity. It has been already argued that the constitutional rights of the House are not directly affected by implied or formally announced arrangements for the sharing of administrative responsibility, provided that clear-cut provisions are made for the allocation of parliamentary questions. Nevertheless there seem to be two potential dangers. The first is the increased opportunity for governmental avoidance of attack at particular, and perhaps critical, moments by transfer of questions from one Minister or department to another. A debate on this practice took place in January 1960, after Opposition complaints to the Speaker that the House had been deprived of an answer before the parliamentary recess by a transfer of questions between the Colonial and Commonwealth Relations Offices. The Speaker declined the invitation to intervene and the Home Secretary asserted that 'The division of responsibility between departments is entirely a matter for the Government and the Prime Minister'.

The second potential danger is that governmental resort to the argument that Ministers as a whole are responsible for policy may ultimately reduce respect given to the House of Commons. Until July 1960, for example, most commentators felt confident in arguing that the obligation to render an account to the Commons would

1. At a ballot of Conservative voters held in February 1959 Mr Nicolson was defeated by 3,762 votes to 3,671 and expressed a willingness to resign.

effectively preclude the appointment of a peer as Foreign Secretary. But, in announcing the appointment of Lord Home, the Prime Minister stated his view that no such necessity existed. In the previous year the Foreign Secretary had, he said, been available for the House to question orally on only five out of twenty-four Foreign Office days. Members need not have 'the full opportunity to question, attack and generally bully-rag the Foreign Secretary'. That had been argued 'as if the whole Government were not answerable to the House of Commons in every department of State'.[1] This argument has become a common one in many spheres. But the immersing of individual in collective responsibility transfers every question to the plane on which a Government may if it wishes refuse explanation, information, or inquiry and proceed to the argument that 'the electorate must judge'. In the face of this answer Oppositions seek satisfaction in vain. The possible culpability of an individual Minister in relation to maladministration in a colonial prison service or to waste and inefficiency in a particular corner of national defence expenditure is treated as a question properly and adequately referable to the verdict of the next General Election. There is nothing novel about this in the context of the modern party situation, but the progressive application of the language of collective responsibility as distinct from its tacit practice deserves to be noted. Moreover, when Ministers offer the collective as a substitute for the individual doctrine it is useful to remember the differences between them. The individual doctrine in its traditional form makes certain assumptions. If A is individually accountable for B it is assumed that the facts about B are either patent or discoverable and that judgments about Ministerial negligence or maladministration can at least in some cases be separated out from judgments reflecting general disagreement about party policy. Neither of these assumptions can be made about the kind of ability or accountability that is associated with a capacity for winning the next General Election.

12. *Administrative policy and specialised committees*

In 1959 the Select Committee on Procedure split on straight party lines on the question of specialised committees for scrutinising the work of departments. Mr R. A. Butler amongst others persuaded the conservative majority that such a system of committees might (in a subtly blended phrase) 'confound the French and American systems'. The Select Committee in its report said that the main argument which had persuaded it to advise adversely on the proposed committee system was that it would constitute a 'radical constitutional

1. 627 HC Deb., 5s., cs. 1995–6.

innovation'. To this the minority, Messrs Wedgwood Benn, Blackburn, Hale, Mitchison, Green and Pannell returned a proper answer: 'Each one of our proposals suggests an innovation; every amendment of the procedure of the House falls within the wide ambit of constitutional law and a large body of opinion believes that reforms should be radical.'

In 1964 Mr Wilson's government took office and in the following May a new Select Committee on Procedure heard evidence in favour of specialised committees. In July the Committee reported[1] that they had been convinced by the argument though they preferred to carry out the scheme by setting up a number of sub-committees of the existing Estimates Committee under broad headings such as Social Services, Defence and Foreign Affairs. The terms of reference, they said, should be 'to examine how the departments of state carry out their responsibilities and to consider their Estimates of Expenditure and Reports'. The efficiency of the Commons would be increased, it was argued, if more information was made available to members about departmental administration. A distinction was made between 'administrative policy' and 'policy questions of political significance'. It was recognised that though the line was difficult to draw in principle, it would be possible to conduct Committee hearings analogous to those of the Select Committee on Nationalised Industries in which wider questions of administration are examined than can be brought within the rubric of financial economy, but without trenching on controversial matters of party or ministerial policy which could not properly be debated with Civil Servants.

The difficulty of defining such matters ahead of time was illustrated by the misgivings expressed in evidence to the Committee of the Head of the Civil Service, Sir Laurence Helsby. Asked to say what areas of government activity he would not want Select Committees to examine, he suggested that any systematic examination of the way in which departments carry out their responsibilities might lead on to inquiry whether certain departments should carry out certain functions at all or whether they would be better carried out by other departments. This would lead into the policy of machinery of government and put Civil Servants in difficulties. The point is a good one since examples given in the minutes of evidence in fact illustrate how the Select Committee's, on the face of it, vague distinction between 'administrative policy' and 'policy questions' can have a reasonable sense attached to it. The question, for example, whether certain management and recruitment functions in the Civil Service are best controlled by the Treasury, is a machinery of government question.

1. HC 303 (1964–5).

So is the question of allocation of functions between the Treasury and the Department of Economic Affairs. But the second in recent times would be an issue of policy in the second more general sense upon which Civil Servants would not be expected to express personal opinions. It does not follow from this that there are not at any time any questions about the machinery of government or allocation of functions which senior Civil Servants can properly discuss with a Select Committee. It is not to be expected that on such occasions Civil Servants who know the minds of their ministers would allow themselves to let fall wildly idiosyncratic personal views.

After the full discussion of these issues before the Select Committee and the Committee's firm recommendation the debate in the House on 27 October was a disappointing one. Mr Bowden for the Government declared himself to be against the widening of the terms of reference of the Estimates Committee and any sub-committees it might set up. The familiar ingredients were stirred well in. Policy was for the House of Commons. The question was whether the House wanted to imitate the American Congressional system. And so on.

The Leader of the House's attitude might perhaps have been divined from his own evidence to the Select Committee. But not that he would carry the Cabinet with him. Nor that his strongest support would come from Mr Michael Foot. Mr Foot's case against specialised committees did not admittedly seem entirely at one with Mr Bowden's. Any Minister worth his salt, he said, could diddle a committee. The view of the Leader of the House, on the other hand, seemed to be that a committee might conceivably diddle a Minister if he chose to appear before it. It would be 'unwise even to risk getting into a position in which the policy of a Department could be examined and investigated.' Asked whether it might have been helpful in the past to have a colonial sub-committee during the emergencies in Kenya or East Africa he replied: 'No, I do not think it would have been at all helpful.' Ministers should never be exposed to such a Committee, he thought, because 'it is a form of detached incisive Question Time. . . . When a Minister could more easily be forced to say things.' Saying things to members should be confined to the floor of the House where pressing queries could be 'dealt with and disposed of'. The Leader of the House appeared to have a poor opinion of Ministers. Neither he nor the Head of the Civil Service seemed to be in total thrall to the vision of parliamentary scrutiny by specialist committee. In mid-1966, however, a further governmental change of mind appeared to have occurred. Committees, it was announced, were to be set up for some domestic departments. But back-benchers were not to be allowed to extend their inquiries to defence or foreign affairs.

Between 1966 and 1969 a number of specialist committees were set up covering Science and Technology, Agriculture (wound up in 1969), Education and Science, Race Relations and Immigration, Scottish Affairs and Overseas Development. The Committees took evidence in public from departmental and outside witnesses. On a number of occasions they also took evidence from Ministers. (During the 1968–9 session Ministers gave evidence on fourteen occasions.) Neither Mr Herbert Morrison nor Mr R. A. Butler, as they then were, would, one feels, have been overjoyed by these exercises.

In 1970 a further procedural rearrangement was proposed. The Estimates Committee was to be converted into an Expenditure Committee with functional sub-committees to consider the activities of the relevant Departments of State 'and to examine the efficiency with which they are administered'.[1] The Nationalised Industries Select Committee and a few other additional subject committees such as Race Relations should also be retained. None of the scrutiny committees appointed since 1966 can confidently be claimed to have made any marked impact on the work of Parliament. A possible exception is, however, the Select Committee on the Parliamentary Commissioner which has been able to exercise a stimulating effect on the operation of the Commissioner and has raised a number of important constitutional queries.

13. *Ministers, Civil Servants and the Parliamentary Commissioner*

An important aspect of the traditional doctrine of ministerial responsibility was the insistence that ministers were entitled, as far as the House of Commons was concerned, to have confidential anonymous advice from their departmental civil servants, whose source they were not obliged to reveal. If it was good advice they took the credit for it and if it was bad advice they accepted the blame. In two ways the operations of the Parliamentary Commissioner system have disturbed the simplicity of this arrangement. For one thing, the Select Committee have interpreted their role as including a duty to discover from the appropriate departmental officers what has been done to put right organisational or procedural faults discovered by the Parliamentary Commissioner's investigations. To carry out this duty they need to take evidence from the appropriate civil servants and have expressed the view that this can be done without undue interference with ministerial–civil servant relationships or hierarchical proprieties. The Wilson Government declined to permit this

1. *Select Committees of the House of Commons* (Cmnd. 4507, 1970).

degree of penetration into the workings of the administration, but there is no doubt that the Committee had the better of the argument.[1] The Committee's conclusion was that the complete anonymity of civil servants need play no part today in the doctrine of ministerial responsibility. The point arises even more urgently when an investigation by the Commissioner reaches the conclusion that particular officers have been guilty of maladministration or that their advice has led to an inappropriate decision. To what extent should such officers or branches be named or blamed. On the one hand (as Mr George Brown argued in 1968 when the Commissioner's report on the Sachsenhausen Concentration Camp compensation case placed responsibility on the Foreign Office officials)[2] the House of Commons had been accustomed to hold ministers responsible for the failings of their departments. On the other hand, Parliament in 1967 deliberately set up an institution designed to discover and report on failings in administration—on who, so to speak, had done what, when and how. If this is done in an adequately detailed way, and if the Select Committee follows up the investigation by public hearings of its own, it is difficult both to preserve anonymity and to prevent the collapse of the fiction of ministerial culpability and control in at least some cases. The result may be a necessary modification in the traditional description of the relations between ministers and civil servants and an increasingly public role for the latter. This may well seem congenial to the spirit of the Fulton Report recommendation[3] favouring more open participation by civil servants in the exposition of policy; but its implications have yet to be worked out.

1. See HC 350 (1967–8).
2. HC 258 (1967–8), pp. ix–xi.
3. The Report concluded that '. . . administration suffers from the convention . . . that only the Minister should explain issues in public. . . . This convention has depended in the past on the assumption that the doctrine of ministerial responsibility means that a Minister has full detailed knowledge and control of all the activities of his department. This assumption is no longer tenable. . . . In our view therefore the convention of anonymity should be modified and civil servants, as professional administrators, should be able to go further than now in explaining what their departments are doing at any rate as far as concerns managing existing policies and implementing legislation.'

The Report adds that 'It is often difficult to explain without appearing to argue' and that 'It would be unrealistic to suppose that a civil servant will not sometimes drop a brick and embarrass his Minister' (Cmnd. 3638, paras. 283–4).

REFERENCES FOR FURTHER READING

THE CONSTITUTION

BAGEHOT, W., *The English Constitution.* Introduction by R. H. S. Crossman (1964 ed.)
DICEY, A. V., *Introduction to the Study of the Law of the Constitution* (10th ed. edited by E. C. S. Wade)
JENNINGS, SIR IVOR, *The Law and the Constitution* (5th ed. 1959)
PHILLIPS, O. HOOD, *Constitutional and Administrative Law* (4th ed. 1967)
WADE, E. C. S., and PHILLIPS, G. G., *Constitutional Law* (7th ed. 1960, ch. 1)
MITCHELL, J. D. B., *Constitutional Law* (2nd ed. 1968)
DE SMITH, S. A., *Constitutional and Administrative Law* (1971)

CONVENTIONS

JENNINGS, SIR IVOR, *Cabinet Government* (3rd ed. 1959, ch. 1)
WHEARE, SIR KENNETH, *Modern Constitutions* (1951, chs. 1, 3 and 8)
WHEARE, SIR KENNETH, *The Constitutional Structure of the Commonwealth* (1960, ch. 1)
HORWILL, H. W., *The Usages of the American Constitution* (1925)
PHILLIPS, O. HOOD, 'Constitutional Conventions: Dicey's Predecessors', *29 Modern Law Review* 137
PHILLIPS, O. HOOD, 'Constitutional Conventions: a Conventional Reply' *Journal of the Society of Public Teachers of Law* (1964–5, p. 60)

THE CROWN

JENNINGS, SIR IVOR, *Cabinet Government* (3rd ed., chs. 3 and 12)
KEITH, A. BERRIEDALE, *The King and the Imperial Crown* (1936)
KEITH, A. BERRIEDALE, *The British Cabinet System* (edited by Gibbs, 1952)
FORSEY, E. A., *The Royal Power of Dissolution of Parliament in the British Commonwealth* (1943)
BASSET, R., *1931: Political Crisis* (1958)
MOODIE, G. C., 'The Monarch and the Selection of a Prime Minister: A Re-examination of the Crisis of 1931', *Political Studies* (1957, vol. 5, p. 1)
MOODIE, G. C., 'The Crown and Parliament', *Parliamentary Affairs* (Summer 1957)
SAMUEL, LORD, 'The Constitutional Crisis of 1931: A Memorandum', *Western Political Quarterly* (March 1959, p. 5)
Correspondence in *The Times* (September 1913 and April 1950)

NICOLSON, SIR HAROLD, *George V: His Life and Reign* (1952)
WHEELER-BENNETT, SIR JOHN, *George VI: His Life and Reign* (1958)
SAINSBURY, K., 'The Constitution—Some Disputed Points', *Parliamentary Affairs* (1963, p. 213)

MINISTERS AND PARLIAMENT

LOW, SIDNEY, *The Governance of England* (1904, chs. 5 and 8)
MORRISON, HERBERT, *Government and Parliament* (1954, chs. 3, 8 and 14)
FINER, S. E., 'The Individual Responsibility of Ministers', *Public Administration* (Winter 1956, p. 377)
CHESTER, D. N., 'The Crichel Down Case', *Public Administration* (Winter 1954, p. 389)
Hansard, *Parliamentary Debates 20 July 1954* (Crichel Down)
MORRIS, A. (Ed.)., *The Growth of Parliamentary Scrutiny by Committee* (1970)
MILNE, R. S., 'The Experiment with Co-ordinating Ministers in the British Cabinet 1951–3', *Canadian Journal of Economics and Political Science* (1955, p. 365)
CHESTER, D. N., and BOWRING, N., *Questions in Parliament* (1962)
BIRCH, A. H., *Representative and Responsible Government* (1964)
MACKINTOSH, J. P., *The British Cabinet* (2nd ed. 1968)
MARSHALL, G., 'Ministerial Responsibility', *Political Quarterly* (1965, p. 256)
CHESTER, D. N., 'The British Parliament 1936–66', *Parliamentary Affairs* (1966, p. 417)
HANSON, A. H., and CRICK, B. (Eds.), *The Commons in Transition* (1970)
FRY, G. K., 'Thoughts on the Present State of the Convention of Ministerial Responsibility', *Parliamentary Affairs* (1969–70, p. 10)

ADMINISTRATIVE JUSTICE

Report of the Committee on Ministers' Powers, Cmnd. 4060 (1932)
Report of the Select Committee on Delegated Legislation, HC 310 (1953)
Report of the Committee on Administrative Tribunals and Enquiries, Cmnd. 218 (1963)
Annual Reports of the Council on Tribunals
Annual Reports of the Parliamentary Commissioner for Administration
GRIFFITH, J. A. G., and STREET, H., *Principles of Administrative Law* (4th ed. 1967)
WADE, H. W. R., *Administrative Law* (3rd ed. 1971)
ALLEN, SIR C. K., *Law and Orders* (3rd ed. 1965)
ROBSON, W. A., *Justice and Administrative Law* (3rd ed. 1951)
DE SMITH, S. A., *Judicial Review of Administrative Action* (2nd ed. 1968)
FRY, G. K., 'The Sachsenhausen Concentration Camp Case and the Convention of Ministerial Responsibility', *Public Law* (1970, p. 336)
CARR, SIR CECIL, 'Parliamentary Control of Delegated Legislation', *Public Law* (Autumn 1956)
ALLEN, SIR C. K., 'Administrative Jurisdiction', *Public Law* (Spring 1958, p. 12)
LAWSON, F. H., 'Dicey Re-visited', *Political Studies* (June and October 1959)
ROBSON, W. A., 'The Franks Report', *Public Law* (Spring–Summer 1958)
Hansard, *Parliamentary Debates 31 October 1957* (The Franks Report) and *3 July 1958* (Tribunals and Inquiries Act)
GRIFFITH, J. A. G., 'The Council and the Chalk Pit', *Public Administration* (1961, vol. 31, p. 369)
WADE, H. W. R., *Towards Administrative Justice* (1963)

WADE, H. W. R., *Constitutional and Administrative Aspects of the Anisminic Case* (1969, 85 LQR 198)
The Citizen and the Administration, A Report by Justice (1961)
YARDLEY, D. C. M., *A Source book of Administrative Law* (2nd ed. 1970)
GARNER, J. F., *Administrative Law* (3rd ed. 1963)
GARNER, J. F., 'The Council on Tribunals', *Public Law* (1965, p. 321)

PARLIAMENTARY PRIVILEGE

EPSTEIN, LEON D., *British Politics and the Suez Crisis* (1964)
DE SMITH, S. A., 'Parliamentary Privilege and the Bill of Rights', *21 Modern Law Review* (1958, p. 465)
THOMPSON, D., 'Letters to Ministers and Parliamentary Privilege', *Public Law* (1959, p. 10)
KILMUIR, VISCOUNT, *The Law of Parliamentary Privilege* (1959)
Hansard, *Parliamentary Debates 4 December 1957* and *8 July 1958*
Reports of the Commons' Committee of Privileges on the cases of Mr Sandys HC 146 (1938), Mr Brown HC 118 (1947), Mr Junor HC 38 (1956–7), Mr Strauss HC 305 (1956–7), Mr Jordan HC 284 (1959–60), Mr Hogg HC 247 (1963–4), Mr Duffy HC 129 (1964–5), Mr Callaghan HC 269 (1964–5), Mr Dalyell HC 357 (1967–8), Essex University HC 308 (1968–9), Mr Maxwell HC 185 (1969–70)
HEUSTON, R. F. V., *Essays in Constitutional Law* (1961, ch. 4)
RICHARDS, P. G., *Honourable Members* (1959, ch. 12)
YARDLEY, D. C. M., 'The House of Commons and its Privileges since the Strauss Affair', *Parliamentary Affairs* (1962, p. 4)
URE, C. SEYMOUR, 'Parliamentary Privilege and Broadcasting', *Parliamentary Affairs* (1962, p. 411)
URE, C. SEYMOUR, 'The Misuse of the Question of Privilege in the 1964–5 Session of Parliament', *Parliamentary Affairs* (1965, p. 380)
URE, C. SEYMOUR, 'Proposed Reforms of Parliamentary Privilege: An Assessment in the Light of Recent Cases', *Parliamentary Affairs* (1970, p. 221)
Select Committee on Broadcasting of Proceedings HC 146 (1966)
Report from the Select Committee on Parliamentary Privilege HC 34 (1968)

INDEX TO CASES

INDEX